Hand to Hand

HAND TO HAND

Listening to the Work of Art

JEAN-LOUIS CHRÉTIEN

Translated with an Introduction
by Stephen E. Lewis

Fordham University Press
New York
2003

Translated from the French edition: *Corps à corps: à l'écoute de l'œuvre d'art* © Editions de Minuit, 1997

Perspectives in Continental Philosophy, No. 32
ISSN 1089-3938

Library of Congress Cataloging-in-Publication Data

Chrétien, Jean-Louis, 1952–
   [Corps á corps. English]
   Hand to hand: listening to the work of art/Jean Louis
Chrétien; translated by Stephen E. Lewis.
      p. cm. — (Perspectives in continental philosophy,
ISSN 1089-3938; no. 32)
      ISBN 0-8232-2289-6 (hard cover:alk.paper)
      ISBN 0-8232-2290-X (pbk.:alk. paper)
      1. Christianity and the arts. 2. Christianity—Philosophy.
3. Arts—Philosophy. I. Title. II. Series.
   BR115.A8C4313   2003
   261.5'7—dc21   2003011118

Printed in the United States of America
07 06 05 04 03 5 4 3 2 1
First English-language edition

For Sébastien

CONTENTS

Translator's Introduction   ix
Stephen E. Lewis

Address   xxv

How to Wrestle with the Irresistible   1

Silence in Painting   18

A Polyptych of Slumbers   62

The Strange Beauty of Charon   81

The Cat as Instrument of Nudity   85

From God the Artist to Man the Creator   94

Like a Liquid Bond   130

Elementary Tears   152

Bibliography   165

Index   179

TRANSLATOR'S INTRODUCTION

Alexandre Kojève's seminar on Hegel's *Phänomenologie des Geistes*, held from 1933–39 at the Ecole des Hautes Etudes in Paris, caught the imagination of a great many French thinkers and writers in their formative years, and as a result left an indelible mark on twentieth-century French philosophical, theoretical, and literary writing.[1] Kojève made Hegel's so-called Master-Slave dialectic the engine of a revamped, existential Marxist vision of history, according to which all violence is perpetually recuperated into progress toward the End of History. As Michael S. Roth has put it, according to this Hegelian vision "history is not merely a slaughterbench, it is the birth of the Truth through the labor of the negative."[2] Most postwar French thinkers that have had a significant readership in the United States—Sartre, Merleau-Ponty, Bataille, Blanchot, Lacan, Foucault, Deleuze, Derrida—struggled in various ways for large portions of their careers with the apparently all-encompassing Hegelian system expounded by Kojève as well as the other major French Hegelians of the 1940s and 1950s, Jean Hyppolite and Eric Weil. These struggles have taken many forms; arguably their most significant effect lies in the widespread belief that tragically violent experience—sometimes meaningful, but more frequently gratuitous and aimless, and thus supposedly incapable of being recuperated into an alienating project—characterizes the living of an authentic human life.

Like a number of his Christian counterparts, Jean-Louis Chrétien offers an alternative to this persistent valorization of tragic violence, which is tragic precisely because it is understood to take place within a horizon of irredeemable death. Chrétien's work constantly appeals to traditions of thought that question the very assumption that experiences of loss, wounding, or falling short are in and of themselves necessarily tragic.[3] The opening essay of *Hand to Hand: Listening to the Work of Art* sets forth the biblical story of Jacob's struggle with the angel, and Delacroix's painterly response to it, as emblematic of an experience of violence wherein, to use one of Chrétien's favorite rhetorical constructions, the chiasmus, the wound blesses and the benediction wounds.[4] As Chrétien shows, Jacob and the nonbelieving Delacroix respond with similar joy to the provocative, unexpected presence of something greater than themselves, which comes upon them from outside: that is, they each unreservedly throw themselves 'body and soul' into intimate struggle with this presence.[5] Such total commitment can result only from an undivided, fearless love of such an encountered presence. Indeed, by Chrétien's account neither Jacob nor Delacroix is divided by self-love or restrained by fear in their respective commitments to intimacy with the combative, irresistible presence that so insistently comes upon them.

Briefly investigating the difference between the struggle Chrétien describes and the Kojévian scenario, on the one hand, and the deconstructive contestation of that scenario carried out by Georges Bataille and Jacques Derrida, on the other, will allow us to place Chrétien's philosophy in relation to some relatively proximate contemporary patterns of thought. A key to the difference lies in what constitutes for each thinker the value and meaning of a life-and-death struggle. In the Kojévian account the "absolute negativity" that operates in a life-and-death encounter, where one or both participants is killed, can never lead to the desired recognition of autonomous human value that occasioned the encounter in the first place. A tragically violent struggle for prestige must therefore be interrupted and the absolute power to negate sublimated into servile work, which gradually transforms the natural world into a place where the recognition of human autonomy can finally take place. Kojève illustrates this circuitous route to the emergence of "autonomous Consciousness-of-self" by a dramatic retelling of Hegel's Master-Slave dialectic in which a bloody battle between two candidates seeking ratification of their humanity is joined, only to be interrupted by the death-fearing surrender of one (the Slave) to the other's (the newly emergent Master's) dominion. A period of forced labor follows, during which the Master experiences dissatisfaction at being recognized as human by someone he himself does not consider to be so, while the Slave, through his servile work, "transform[s] the World [. . . and in so doing] transforms himself [by differentiating himself from the World of Nature] and thus creates the new objective conditions that allow him to take up again the liberatory Struggle for recognition that he had at first refused out of fear of death."[6] By being forced on pain of death to work upon the material of the world to satisfy the master's desires, says Kojève, the slave himself gradually becomes a master of nature. His work liberates him from his own nature, which he had assumed in obeying the instinct for preservation and refusing to fight to the death. By becoming, through work, a master of nature, the slave liberates his own nature as initially defined by his fear of death at the hands of his opponent, and eventually reaches a point where he can free himself from the master. The force of death is absorbed by the slave's fear and thus transformed into a productive force, gradually emerging through the work of the slave's hands to negate nature and in the process build up sense and meaning that the slave will ultimately grasp in self-consciousness. "Thus it is the initially dependent, serving, and servile Consciousness that realizes and reveals in the end the ideal of the autonomous Consciousness-of-self, and that is thus its 'truth.'"[7]

Jacques Derrida follows Georges Bataille in objecting to the way in which the Kojévian account of the dialectical sublimation of the power of death (the famous *Aufhebung*) renders that power safe for reason by making it serve the emergence of autonomous self-consciousness.[8] Bataille's deconstructive ("sovereign") textual strategies, says Derrida, trace instants of "sacred" experience that belie the Hegelian conviction that death can be so tidily put to work in order to make sense. Bataille's strategies unmask the fear of death that, in this account, lies behind Hegel's resort to the *Aufhebung*, and, by "miming" "heedless sacrifice" (the "absolute negativity" that Kojève says must be sublimated), allow the power of death in all of its sovereign meaninglessness to erupt momentarily into experience. Derrida writes:

> To be indifferent to the comedy of the *Aufhebung*, as was Hegel, is to blind oneself to the experience of the sacred, to the heedless sacrifice of presence and meaning. Thus is sketched out a figure of experience . . . *displaced* in phenomenology of mind, like laughter in philosophy, and which mimes through sacrifice the absolute risk of death. Through this mime it simultaneously produces the risk of absolute death, the feint through which this risk can be lived, the impossibility of reading a sense or a truth in it, and the laughter which is confused, in the simulacrum, with the opening of the sacred.[9]

Bataille's writing, says Derrida, mimes a death that is paradoxically constructed to be at once the most concrete and the most unknowable reality. Bataille's mimicry of "heedless sacrifice" contests Hegel's rejection of killing as "abstract negativity" by "mak[ing] the seriousness of meaning [rescued from death by the dialectic] appear as an abstraction inscribed in play."[10]

The story of Jacob's struggle with the angel testifies to an entirely different understanding of death, and thus of life. For Derrida and Bataille, death as a personal event is impossible to think of.[11] There is no one outside me who can teach me anything fundamental about my death, or about my life;

and every experience I conceive as analogous to the experience of my death is only a mere simulacrum of what, from the point of view of life as self-conscious self-sufficiency, is always already assumed to be a total loss. Despite their differences, both Hegelian and Bataillean / Derridean anthropology are characterized by what Chrétien calls an "obsession" with "the human project of total self-assurance and self-understanding . . . in transparency."[12] Jacob, by contrast, struggles as a mortal who is relatively free of this obsession, and thus as one who lives convinced of the likelihood that something or someone outside him could fundamentally transform his life. Jacob's freedom is "rooted at each instant in listening to an other Word that," precisely because it is anterior to any project of self-understanding in transparency (for example, strategic plans for the morrow's encounter with Esau), "wounds body and soul."[13] Such listening is dramatic, fully implicated in what it hears: Jacob's struggle becomes "amorous" precisely because his relationship to his own life is not primarily conceptual (dialectical or contestatory), but rather determined by his relationship to another. Within this relationship of loving exchange, the very death brought about through its violence is the occasion for new life. Describing Delacroix's depiction of Jacob disencumbered of his weapons as he wrestles, Chrétien writes,

> To give up all defenses and weapons in order to enter into the fight, to confront the irresistible assailant counting on nothing more than one's own presentation, to come at him openly: such are the conditions of combats that are in truth matters of life and death, combats in which something of ours must die, and a new life enter to dwell within us. Only the disarmed can grow in strength. To take arms, to surround oneself with defenses, is already to place oneself in a position of weakness, and at the same time to refuse the salutary intimacy of close combat. What must die in us will only truly die by not allowing itself to die, by burning up every last bit of its power, without any reserve. This is what it means to die a natural death.[14]

The French in the penultimate sentence—*brûlant sans réserve toute sa puissance mise à nu et à vif*—echoes a typical Bataillean locution (*brûler sans réserve*) that is echoed in the subtitle to Derrida's essay on Bataille (*un hegelianisme sans réserve*). But the life-and-death combat described here by Chrétien differs significantly from the tragicomic, "sacrificial" mimicry described by Bataille. For Jacob, a life-and-death struggle can truly be characterized as an experience of life-giving "salutary intimacy" with another; for Bataille the joy in such a struggle is found only in the despairing experience of my own mortal anguish.[15] The combat described by Chrétien culminates in a "communication of force" where "confrontation becomes exchange," rather than an "annihilation of the force of the other" (however joyful for the victim such annihilation could be imagined to be).[16] Jacob and Delacroix each exemplify in their active self-abandonment to amorous struggle with the unexpected other the "mysterious lameness" that characterizes the human ontological constitution according to Judeo-Christian thought.[17] For Jacob, the blow to the hip from the infinite breaks open his human finitude and dilates it, giving him a new name and more abundant life. Similarly Delacroix, in embracing as his own the irresistible, "dizzying possibility" described by the Biblical text, exhausts the final years of his life in the effort to meet the imperious demands of his work, effort that results in a mural painting whose "trenchant light . . . shows" the dramatic source of its energy "without adorning or comparing" (6, 10). Chrétien's ekphrasis and analysis of Delacroix's Chapel of the Angels demonstrates that the painting succeeds because it embroils the viewer in the very drama out of which it was made: the painting testifies to the "burn" of a presence (xxvi) left upon the one who made it, and offers to the viewer the blessings of a similar wound. "*Nihil sufficit animae, nisi ejus capacitatem excedat,*" "Nothing suffices for the soul but that which exceeds its capacity":

when human embodied life responds with love to the irresistible assault of what is greater, it is, from within its very finitude, creatively enriched and expanded, rather than torn apart and destroyed.[18]

The claim that Delacroix's painting is successful implies a criterion of judgment by which such success is to be measured. One of the most interesting features of Chrétien's account of the positive, life-giving violence witnessed to by the story of Jacob and the angel is his often subtly stated yet robustly critical account of what a good painting, or a good poem, is and does. The centrality of a dramatic, intimate relationship with what is outside our self-understanding—another person, beauty—figures importantly here too. To understand Chrétien's evaluative account of the success of the art work, we need to understand first how he conceives of the work of art in its essence.

In his "Address" to the reader, Chrétien tells us that *Hand to Hand* constitutes "a dialogue with works and what they look upon," and that each work of art (visual or verbal) considered in the book is a "manual act of presence (drawing, painting, writing)" formed in response to the appeal seen and heard by the artist in the "acts of presence" made by human bodies (xxv). Chrétien assumes here, and especially in the essay "Silence in Painting," what he has shown at length in his book *L'Appel et la réponse:* that the call of beauty appeals to the entire body, so that we are absolutely accurate to say, with Paul Claudel, that the eye listens to and the ear sees the presence of beauty. "The call [appel]," writes Chrétien, "is anterior to the notion of sign, for it is the condition of possibility for its constitution." [19] The dynamic of call (or appeal) and response constitutes a path of continual antiphonal movement; thus we should understand Chrétien's careful ekphrastic translations of each of the individual works he discusses in *Hand to Hand* as necessarily taking their place within this dynamic, as does, in turn, our reading.[20]

Chrétien approaches the work as an existential phenomenon rather than a generic object in relationship to norms
of representation, figuration, or abstraction, all of which
are in Chrétien's view secondary to the essence of painting.
(In this respect, Chrétien's approach to art shares aspects of
the approaches of Maurice Merleau-Ponty, Henri
Maldiney, and Michel Henry.)[21] Such an approach allows
for qualitative distinctions between paintings in terms of
whether or not a work is true to its phenomenal nature,
which is to say, fashioned in accordance with rather than in
opposition to the fact that it is the translation into forms of
a human act of listening that in its turn gives itself to be lis-
tened to (57). Human beings make paintings in response to
the "musical silence" of the world; when we look at a good
painting, this silence is given to us to hear.

Why then do we not always hear this silence? Sometimes,
says Chrétien, the fault lies with the painting; at other times,
with the listener. Listening is never a solitary activity; to
take place, two silences must meet and respond to one
another. "It is with *our* silence that we listen to the silence in
painting: two antiphonic silences, two silences that respond
to one another, give one another a fresh start, and in a certain sense embrace one another" (19). A painting can be
"chatty" (*bavarde*), as can a viewer.[22] This, essentially, is the
charge that Chrétien, at the end of the essay "Silence in
Painting," levels against Georges Bataille's approach to
painting. We appreciate here again an implicit continuity
between the essays that make up Chrétien's book: the fullness of human existence is best described as a dramatic listening to what comes to us from outside our projects of
self-understanding. Bataille, says Chrétien, drowns out the
sound in painting with a "metaphysical thesis," arguing
that Manet's work inaugurates a definitive, yet "impossible," rupture with discursivity in painting (56). Such
"apophatic, acosmic" (54) arguments about an artist's
impossible break with discursivity—impossible because, to
be known, the break must be articulated discursively—have

driven an entire generation or two of American academic writing about literature and art. They are anchored in the conviction that only the tragic violence of a double bind—another permutation of the obsession with self-understanding in transparency—marks advanced thinking.

Chrétien's alternative to such arguments is to show that the discursive-nondiscursive binary upon which they are based is of secondary importance (if indeed it exists at all)[23] to the fact that human acts of presence are essentially responsive, always already inhabited by a presence that precedes and creates them. If we accept this demonstration, coherence requires us to respond with hospitality to the silence that calls us (163). Chrétien's judgments of paintings that respond to the phenomena of bodies that are sleeping or nude hinge upon the degree to which such works offer a view that is hospitable to whatever it is in these bodies that is secret, unmasterable, or invisible (78). Insofar as an ethical judgment is at issue here, it is one that is indexed to a determination of fact. Bad painting and bad poetry, as well as bad writing about painting and poetry, fail in similar ways to see and to listen to *events* (93). They deal in bodies that "do not exist," bodies that, in their total availability to spectatorship, no longer bear breath (78). They deal either in what is merely "mythological," or in what is dead (85).

For Chrétien, the primacy of the event guarantees the drama of existence. Elsewhere, Chrétien compares Jacob's "amorous contest" with the angel to prayer.[24] In prayer, speech or a "manual act of presence" itself becomes an event. This is what Chrétien in *L'Arche de la parole* calls the "*dramatique de la parole*," the drama of speech.[25] The "manual acts of presence" we make in response to the in-breaking (*effraction*) or advent of beauty are good and true acts when they are offered as acts of adoration. A true response to beauty emerges out of the very desire opened by its taking place. To pretend to speak about the event of beauty from a stance of spectatorial overview, as if one had not been touched by its taking place, is to deny the very gift of that desire.[26] An excellent example of dramatic speech occurs in *Hand to Hand* when, concerning Delacroix's essentially responsive approach to the story of Jacob and the angel, Chrétien writes, "The founding events of sacred history do not cease to write and prolong themselves in new existences. . . . They never finish taking place, if we offer them this place that is our life. Why does Jacob matter, if we cannot become him? Why does his angel matter, if he no longer has the force to assault us? What does this combat matter, if it cannot take place this very night?" (8). These words do not argue from a point outside the drama they describe. Instead, they recall events that have taken place, give an imminent account of how they happened and go on happening, and issue an invitation to participate in their continued happening.[27]

Yet the stance of spectatorial pretense before beauty is virtually everywhere adopted in present-day Western culture. Why? In the essay "From God the Artist to Man the Creator" Chrétien shows how key decisions regarding the relationship between the work, the artist, and God occurring within the tradition of Christian Platonism have contributed decisively to the rise and subsequent dominance of the modern spectatorial overview. Despite our best efforts, Chrétien writes, "from the moment that the artistic analogy [comparing God to an artist] unfolds within thinking about the creative act and the relation of God to the world," the dissimilarity originally included in the artistic analogy between God as artist and man as artist fades, and man stands before God as a "creator," in a "relationship of connivance" rather than of praise (120, 119). Though he never argues a cause and effect relationship, Chrétien shows clearly that the fading of this strong sense of the dissimilarity between God and man, commonly held in both ancient Greek and non-Augustinian Christian thinking, coincides with a turn away from the Christological thinking that, in the work of such Christian Platonists as Saint

Augustine and Saint Bonaventure, constantly recalls this dissimilarity (120). When it ceases to be a dramatic response to the presence of Jesus Christ, theological thinking, and especially analogical theological thinking, tends to develop a 'natural' anthropology, and to conceive of a God lacking in divinity.

This important essay is somber in tone, indeed at times severely pessimistic about the possibility that contemporary men and women might once again attend to the dramatic role of the human hand in human making. But the overall effect of *Hand to Hand* inspires hope in no small part because it exemplifies what it describes. The book demonstrates the intellectual and spiritual power of dramatic speech to sidestep the labor of the negative and to speak a 'yes' to the excess of the call over every response. Like Paul Claudel's saturating and thoroughly saturated *"laudes aquae"* (subject of the book's penultimate essay), Jean-Louis Chrétien's written words in *Hand to Hand* translate phenomenal experience and, at the same time, offer themselves as phenomena that witness to the continual transfiguration of human corporeal life by new possibilities. The ultimate source and goal of these possibilities is evident for those who "have ears," for what Chrétien says of Claudel's dramatic speech seems descriptive of his own *parole*, as well: "There can never be a question concerning God, nor our relation to God, nor the relation of God to us, without the Incarnation of God in Christ being present as at once both the center and the horizon of this word" (143). Chrétien's word tells us that, in the loving encounter with the One who exceeds us, every defeat can become a victory because the human being has been given the ability to speak from and within the memory of the event of Jesus Christ.

STEPHEN E. LEWIS
The Lumen Christi Institute, Chicago
January 2003

NOTES

1. Vincent Descombes offers an excellent account of the influence of Kojève's interpretation of Hegel's *Phenomenology* on subsequent French philosophy in his book *Modern French Philosophy*, 9–54, 112–14, 137–41, 158–61; see also Descombes' essay "La crise française des lumières," in *Philosophie par gros temps*, 69–95.

2. Roth, *Knowing and History*, 197. Among those who attended the seminar were Raymond Aron, Georges Bataille, André Breton, Henry Corbin, Gaston Fessard, Jacques Lacan, Maurice Merleau-Ponty, Raymond Queneau, and Eric Weil. Kojève's teachings were assembled into book form by Queneau and published after the war: see Kojève, *Introduction à la lecture de Hegel*.

3. Chrétien, "Retrospection," 126. Chrétien makes an explicit comment on Kojève's interpretation of Hegel in a critique of Maurice Blanchot's appropriation and curious development of the Kojévian interpretation of naming as murder; see Chrétien, *L'Arche de la parole*, 6–9. Elsewhere in his millennial "Retrospection" Chrétien describes his attempts "to show that certain themes that contemporary thought has sometimes believed itself to initiate are in fact already present and alive in the ancient traditions" (125). *Hand to Hand: Listening to the Work of Art* employs the ancient sources—primarily Platonic—as well as the Biblical, patristic, and seventeenth-century French Catholic mystical sources found often in Chrétien's earlier as well as subsequent work; but also present in *Hand to Hand* are many modern, especially poetic and artistic, sources. Similar convictions about the usefulness of ancient thought in approaching contemporary problems animate Catherine Pickstock's work in *After Writing*, Part I of which argues against a perceived postmodern projection of modern tragic violence onto Platonic thought. Jean-Luc Marion has worked in a similar spirit, making extensive use of the Biblical distinction between idols and icons to intervene at numerous points in contemporary discussions about God, ontotheology, and givenness (cf. Marion, *The Idol and Distance, God Without Being, Being Given,* and *In Excess*). Also in Marion (although not an appeal to ancient thought) we find a particularly vivid, nontragic alternative to the Kojévian struggle scenario: love is described as a "crossing of gazes," which "imitates the crossing of swords—what [the lovers] each see of the other consists in the balanced tension of aims, like two weapons crossed" (see Marion, *Prolegomena to Charity*, 89).

4. Chrétien, "Retrospection," 122.

5. A French expression to describe such unrestrained struggle is *"à corps perdu,"* one of many expressions in the French language that uses the word "corps" when English would employ some other or additional word. The French title of this book—*Corps à corps: à l'écoute de l'œuvre d'art*—contains another such expression. *"Corps à corps,"* which literally means "body to body," is used in French (as in Italian and Spanish) to describe what in English is called "hand-to-hand" fighting—thus in French Chrétien describes Jacob's wrestling with the angel as *"une lutte corps à corps."* The emphasis on the hand in the idiom of the English title for this book (which was approved by the author) certainly mutes the original French title's emphasis on the role of the entire body as site of response to the call; yet, perhaps felicitously, the English idiom calls attention to Chrétien's beautiful description of the grappling hands in Delacroix's "Jacob and the Angel" that concludes the first essay, as well as the author's emphasis on the importance of the hand found in the final pages of the important essay "From God the Artist to Man the Creator."

6. Kojève, *Introduction*, 34, my translation. All translations are my own unless otherwise indicated.

7. Ibid.

8. Derrida's thought has of course developed in many ways since the 1967 publication of *Writing and Difference* (the book that contains Derrida's principal essay on Bataille). Yet Derrida's recent work contains patterns of thought that very much resemble those present in the 1967 book. For instance, his critical discussion in *Donner la mort* of the demonic, its supposed two-stage disciplinary *"refoulement"* or "sacrifice" in Platonism and Christianity, and the subsequent emergence of European responsibility bears striking structural similarities to his valorization of Bataille's critical engagement with the Hegelian dialectic (Derrida, *Donner la mort*, note in particular 24 and 29 for the emergence of Hegelian language despite the focus on Patočka's Heideggerianism).

9. Derrida, "De l'économie," 378; tran. Bass, *Writing and Difference*, 256 [translation slightly modified].

10. Derrida, "De l'économie," 377; tran. Bass, *Writing and Difference*, 256.

11. As an example, see the passage from Bataille's *Méthode de méditation*, quoted by Derrida, "De l'économie," 406; tran. Bass, *Writing and Difference*, 276. Chrétien shows elsewhere that philosophical claims about the impossibility of thinking about death tend to result from a refusal to think seriously about immortality, and thus of death as a power belonging to the human being. Following Saint Augustine, Chrétien shows that this important feature of human agency—the power to die and the power not to die—can only be thought about coherently, in all of its valences, if mortality and immortality are understood in relation to one another. See Chrétien's essay "Pouvoir mourir et devoir mourir selon la théologie chrétienne," 165–204. I refer here most immediately to 168, but the entire essay is pertinent. The power to die or not to die seems an obscured yet fundamental question in Bataille's thought; the precise meaning and status of suicide, in particular, is unclear in relation to the practice of certain contestatory acts that, as Derrida puts it, "mime" "sacrifice." See Ernst, *Georges Bataille*, 25–27, 94–104 for an enlightening discussion of the questionable status and meaning of suicide in Bataille's work.

12. Chrétien, "Retrospection," 123.

13. Chrétien, "Retrospection," 125.

14. Jean-Louis Chrétien, *Corps à corps: à l'écoute de l'œuvre d'art (Hand to Hand: Listening to the Work of Art)* (Paris: Les Editions de Minuit, 1997), 14–15. Further citations to the translated text will be given parenthetically in the Introduction.

15. "Gaiety, connected with the work of death, causes me anguish, is accentuated by my anguish, and in return exacerbates that anguish: ultimately, gay anguish, anguished gaiety cause me, in a feverish chill, 'absolute dismemberment,' where it is my joy that finally tears me apart, but where dejection would follow joy were I not torn all the way to the end, immeasurably." Bataille, *Œuvres complètes*, XII:342; translated into English as "Hegel, Death and Sacrifice," 25; quoted by Derrida, "De l'économie," 380; tran. Bass, *Writing and Difference*, 259.

16. Chrétien, *Hand to Hand*, 4. For Bataille, true sacrifice is "un sacrifice où tout est victime," in which "le sacrificateur lui-même est touché par le coup qu'il frappe, il succombe et se perd avec sa victime" (a sacrifice in which everything is a victim . . . the sacrificer himself is hit by the same blow that he strikes, he succumbs and is lost with his victim). Bataille, *L'expérience intérieure* in *Œuvres complètes*, V:175, 176.

17. Lubac, *Le mystère du surnaturel*, 149; tran. Sheed, *The Mystery of the Supernatural*, 113–14.

18. Saint Bonaventure, *Quaestiones disputatae de scientia Christi*, VI, quoted in Chrétien, *Le regard de l'amour*, 247.

19. Chrétien, *L'Appel et la réponse*, 18. For the full argument, see the book's first two essays: "L'Appel et la réponse," 15–44, and "La Voix visible," 45–56.

20. Chrétien's ekphrasis exemplifies the work of translation that he says necessarily takes place in every act of listening to the manifestation (call and appeal) of beauty. For more on Chrétien's understanding of response as translation (mentioned in *Hand to Hand*, 57), see *L'Appel et la réponse*, 58, 88–89, and Chrétien, "La traduction irréversible," 309–28. In this latter text, Chrétien writes, "Le premier dire est déjà *traduction*, notre écoute fait toujours déjà de nous un *truchement*. . . . La parole commence par traduire" (The first saying is already *translation*, our listening makes us always already an *interpreter*. . . . Speech begins with translation [328]).

21. Merleau-Ponty wrote famously of painting in *L'Œil et l'esprit:* "It is impossible to say that here nature ends and the human being or expression begins. It is, then, silent Being that itself comes to show forth its own meaning. Herein lies the reason why the dilemma between figurative and nonfigurative art is wrongly posed; it is at once true and uncontradictory that no grape was ever what it is in the most figurative painting and that no painting, no matter how abstract, can get away from Being, that even Caravaggio's grape is the grape itself. This precession of what is upon what one sees and makes seen, of what one sees and makes seen upon what is—this is vision itself" (Merleau-Ponty, *L'Œil et l'esprit*, 87; tran. Smith, "Eye and Mind," 147). Similar points of view can be found in Maldiney, *Regard, Parole, Espace*, for example, 250 (a passage mentioned in *Hand to Hand*, 63), and in Henry, *Voir l'invisible: Sur Kandinsky*, for example, 221–24. For a critical map of the vast number of philosophical studies of painting written in France during the last twenty-five years, see Mongin, *Face au scepticisme (1976–1993)*, 206–11. We can lengthen Mongin's list to include works by Alain Besançon and Jean-Marie Schaeffer, among others, if we extend it to 1997, the French publication date of *Hand to Hand*.

22. In the essay "L'hospitalité du silence," in *L'Arche de la parole*, Chrétien describes *"la parole du bavardage,"* chatty speech, as "speech that . . . gives no silence at all to hear, and gives to silence nothing of the light it might have shed" (59). Chrétien writes that *Hand to Hand*'s "Silence in Painting" "completes" this essay (57 n. 1).

23. Cf. Chrétien's suspicion that the radical nothingess limned "impossibl[y]" by the apophatic language of the late Greek philosopher Damascius, "the greatest 'deconstructor' in the history of philosophy," may "still be an all too human representation, the emptiness of our own mind transfigured into an idol" (Ibid., 94, 96).

24. Chrétien, "La prière selon Kierkegaard," 115; see also *L'Arche*, 127.

25. *L'Arche*, 123.

26. *L'Arche*, 131.

27. Chrétien speaks in similar fashion of Georges De La Tour's painting *L'Adoration des bergers* (*Hand to Hand*, 48), and of several painterly treatments of the sleep of the apostles at Gethsemane (66). In each of these three cases, Chrétien also appeals to seventeenth-century French mystical authors for keys to interpreting both the paintings and the phenomena to which they respond, namely, Jacob's wrestling, the silence of the *verbum infans*, and the retreat of the disciples into sleep, respectively. The approach of the French mystics is always dramatic, and obviously an inspiration for Chrétien's own writing.

Address

BODIES THAT EMBRACE in order to wrestle, or wrestle in order to embrace; bodies that with every fiber listen to, or play, invisible or visible music; bodies that fall asleep due to sadness, drunkenness, or serenity; bodies that strip themselves; bodies that swim through various media; bodies that mingle their tears with those of the sea—such are the phenomena that the pages your gaze has just begun to notice advance to meet. A shared restlessness inhabits and moves across their diversity—the sort of joyous restlessness that pushes our feet forward, and causes our eyes to rise again and our hearts to beat. The fact that the body alone witnesses to the spirit, and endlessly sends us letters of credence, or of apostasy and repudiation, is enough to guarantee the inexhaustible character of the spirit's manifestations and to keep us awake to them. These manifestations call forth speech, which gathers up meaning from them to translate itself there and catch its breath, incessantly.

At issue here will be these manifestations, treated in antiphonic, which is to say alternating, fashion, according to the response or rather the responses that the silently speaking hands of painters and the secretly lucid voices of poets give them, delivering or transmitting these manifestations to us, through and within this very response. A photographic foray aside, the studies that follow are in fact devoted to painting and, to a lesser extent, poetry. Yet, the point here is neither art history nor esthetics, but rather a dialogue with the works and with what they look upon. In responding by a manual act of presence (drawing, painting, writing—which in Greek are the same word, *graphein*)

to bodily acts of presence, in delivering over to verbal or
plastic form that of the spirit which comes to attest to itself
in them, poetry and painting do not procure for us new
objects to consider, but rather a new source of ɪ ˈessness.

Their response in turn calls for us to respond, ː ʊ that the
burn of the visible that aroused that response might not go
out in us or heal over. Here in this book, this response is
written: there will be no images, no "reproductions"—the
intention being not to take the place of the works, but to
issue from them and to address them. It is given manually,
without there being a final touch, any more than there is a
first touch. This is why the antepenultimate study leaves off
from staying close to the works in order to attempt, in a
more historical mode, a genealogy of the notion of *creator*,
insofar as it has come to be applied to the artist. This decision of transferal was a serious one, and the consequences
continue to affect us. Perhaps this decision involves a forgetting of the hand, and of its dignity. If yours continues to
hold this book, you will have understood that this is hardly
a preface or an introduction, but simply an address, a
directive for continuing along the way, itself in transit. It
passes on, and so do you. May you find the light favorable!

Paris, September 1996

Hand to Hand

How to Wrestle with the Irresistible

THERE ARE VICTORIES that weigh heavily and overpower. There are also defeats that revive, where new, unlooked-for strengths spring forth suddenly from the wounds received. To his misfortune, king Pyrrhus attached his name to costly victories: Plutarch tells us that he "responded to one who was rejoicing with him over the victory he had won: 'If we win another for that price, we will be completely ruined,'" while his Roman adversaries "in no way lost heart at the few losses they had sustained, but exerted themselves so much the more, and proclaimed angrily for the continuation of this war."[1] And it is not only in war that we are weakened by our successes and increased by our falls. Who is unaware of this?

It is a fine thing to seek out fitting adversaries, rather than those whom we have already defeated by sight before even engaging in a struggle. But it is an even finer thing to receive an adversary who *exceeds* our measure, an irresistible adversary, for where else might we deploy ourselves to the unknown ends of our strength? A wonderful poem by Rilke, in the *Book of Images,* says it with a lively simplicity. After having meditated on the scars left upon the trees by storms, Rilke writes:

> How small that is, with which we wrestle,
> what wrestles with us, how immense[2]

This dissymmetry puts into play nothing other than the break between initiative and sudden shock, between that which we go toward, having chosen and measured it, and that which, having elected us, comes upon us and surprises us. Rilke continues:

> What we triumph over is the Small,
> and the success itself makes us petty.
> The Eternal and Unexampled
> *will* not be bent by us.

Such is the "angel" who "appeared to the wrestlers of the Old Testament." And the final stanza makes explicit, yet without his name ever being uttered, the allusion to Jacob's grappling with the angel.

> Whomever this Angel overcame
> (who so often declined the fight),
> *he* walks erect and justified
> and great out of that hard hand
> which, as if sculpting, nestled round him.
> Winning does not tempt him.
> His growth is: to be the deeply defeated
> by ever greater things.

Sein Wachstum ist: der Tiefbesiegte / von immer Größerem zu sein. There are wounds in which we find satisfaction, and that we maintain and deepen with our moans and our morose delight, savoring our weakness. They need not even be cared for; one must simply leave them, forget about them, for they will heal over on their own, because they exist only to be looked at, told about, recalled to mind. And then there are wounds that one must not heal, for they are the source of our loving intimacy with our highest task, the one we have received, impossibly, without having sought it.

Jacob is forever the eponym of such wounds, a strange eponym, because in the course of the very struggle with the angel during which he was finally wounded, he also received a change of name, becoming Israel from that point forward. Eponym of the highest struggle, he is thus in addition the eponym of the name lost and found, the eponym of changes of name insofar as this struggle left nothing of his existence intact, neither body nor identity, insofar then as the event of the intimate confrontation is also the advent of an unforeseen and new intimacy. Jacob needed a displaced hip, an uncertain gait from that point forward, in order to receive his most secure name, the one no man would ever have been able to give him. This scene, among the most mysterious in the Holy Bible, nevertheless turns toward each of us its clear and open face. Who among us has not known such a night? Or who has not fled from one, regardless of the cost, which still entails having had to recognize the peril that comes out to meet us in such a night?

After having helped his entire family and all of his possessions across the ford of the Jabbok, "Jacob stayed alone." It is in this nocturnal solitude that the closest partner that a man might have comes, out of his very own initiative and without Jacob's having been able to expect it or prepare himself, to find and assault him.

> And there was one that wrestled with him until day break who, seeing that he could not master him, struck him in the socket of his hip, and Jacob's hip was dislocated as he wrestled with him. He said, "Let me go, for day is breaking." But Jacob answered, "I will not let you go unless you bless me." He then asked, "What is your name?" "Jacob," he replied. He said, "Your name shall no more be called Jacob, but Israel, for you have striven with God and with men, and have prevailed." Jacob then made this request, "I beg you, reveal to me your name," but he replied, "Why do you ask my name?" And he blessed him there.[3]

The one who gives a new name does not himself give his own name. The one who threw himself upon Jacob is the one who wants to interrupt the hand-to-hand fighting. The angel of blessings asks for a favor, and Jacob does not grant it, for it is blessing and favor that he himself wants to receive. The strongest is at the point of allowing himself to be beaten by the weakest. And Jacob does not fight to throw his adversary, but to obtain a word, a word of benediction, and though he had to hear it at the cost of never again being able to walk straight by himself and on his own, he will depart with this benediction upon him. Who is the victor? Who is the vanquished?

The mystery and the paradoxes of this scene have given rise to multiple, sometimes contradictory, interpretations in the religious tradition. The narrative clearly forbids a negative account, for one does not ask for a benediction from evil powers. Philo of Alexandria, great Jewish thinker that he was, insists rightly on the grappling, to the point of naming Jacob "the athlete." The divine word, he writes, "summons him to the exercises, then closes with him and forces him to wrestle until it has developed in him an irresistible strength (anantagôniston)."[4] This grappling is an embrace, in which the irresistible seeks to render Jacob irresistible, and succeeds. This combat is not about an annihilation of the force of the other, but rather a communication of force. Is it not true that, in certain struggles, there comes a time when the force that assaults can no longer be distinguished from that which holds out? Or when the confrontation becomes an exchange?

Pursuing his athletic comparison, Philo sees in Jacob's hip wound "the crown of the victor," "a guerdon the most wondrous of all awards ever announced in honour of a victor."[5] For Philo, to allow oneself to be outstripped by what is better than oneself is the wound of humility, the loving wound, sincerely desired and accepted. No one is stronger than when he gives place in such a way to that which surpasses him, without, however, consenting to separate himself from it, but, instead, following it and pursuing it with a limping step. "His apparent defeat will be a victory."[6] Thus, thanks to this dislocation of the hip, says another of Philo's treatises, "the inordinate strength of the passions may be exhausted and thus provide a breadth in which the better part of the soul may expand."[7] In this struggle of Jacob with the angel, the Christian authors will often see a chiaroscuro prefiguration of the incarnation.[8] When at the end of his poem Rilke underlines that, in such a combat, to be defeated elevates, because allowing oneself to be beaten supposes that one has defeated oneself, and thus to a certain extent surpassed oneself thanks to the excess of force come from the other, he places himself in the purest and most vital theological tradition. Seventeenth-century French spirituality had an acute awareness of this grappling with God, and described it forcefully. It is worthwhile to quote certain passages that are as beautiful as they are forgotten, and of difficult access.

For Saint François de Sales, we are each new Jacobs, assaulted by God, and his perseverance should be for us a constant source of confidence. He writes in a letter:

No: Our Lord may turn us and sweep us round to the left or to the right; he may, as if with other Jacobs, clasp us tightly, and wrench us in a hundred ways; he may press us first to one side, then to the other; in short, he may do us a thousand hurts; nevertheless we will not leave him until he has given us his eternal blessing. And let me add, my daughter, that our good God only abandons us in order better to secure us; never does he leave us except to watch over us all the more; never does he wrestle with us except in order to give himself to us and to bless us.[9]

Jacob forms not a moral example, but a properly religious example. He summons up for us not a law, but the paradox of faith. To unfold its movements, love's violence has as much need of the faraway as it does the close-up. Love lights up the proximate within the faraway to continue to be love; and love opens the faraway in the proximate to continue to be an approach, and the sudden shock of an approach, an everyday, common miracle. The most beautiful page ever written on this loving struggle was composed by Louis Chardon, a great Dominican mystic and a wonderful writer. Judge for yourself:

God appeared to him, not in order to unfold in his breast the outpouring of the comforts of his Providence, like before, but in order to make him experience its rigors. He first treats him like an enemy. He seizes him about the body to hurl him to the ground; he shakes him, jolts him, strikes him. It appears that the outcome of this rough attack will be the end of Jacob's life. In truth, he soon finds himself reduced to the last extremities of agony, hard-pressed by the force of the assailant, seized with terror at so brusque and unforeseen an arrival of this Omnipotence who fights without giving warning, who redoubles his attack before one has the means to go on the defensive, and who wants to carry off the victory without giving his competitor a chance to glory in the knowledge that he was vanquished by the One to whom he owes his being and his life.

Nevertheless, Jacob, instead of drawing despair from a combat begun with so much heat between unequal parties, is roused to confidence. His antagonist's holds reassure him. His grasps and grips swell his courage. His approaches fortify him. His joltings strengthen him more and more. This war begins to please Jacob, solely because the combatants seek union rather than separation from one another. This is why they embrace one another, grip and clasp one another, and why the most valiant is the one whose accolades are ever tighter, so that, hold for hold, he fastens himself to his adversary with such perseverance that no effort the adversary might exert upon him could cause him to give up the fight. The blow that he gives to him on the thigh, causing him a fresh pain, is favorable, because in losing the strength in his leg to hold himself up, he is forced to redouble the efforts of his grasping in order better to steady himself. It is nevertheless true that, if he were not held up by the One who, in clasping him, communicates to him his omnipotence, he would not have held out long enough to overcome the Omnipotent.[10]

Who could retell such a story without himself being wounded? Who could return intact from such an encounter? It contains a possibility so vertiginous that no one could even glimpse it, if indeed he truly glimpses it, without falling toward and into it. Even a nonbelieving painter could not paint the struggle between Jacob and the angel with impunity. Such was the fate of Delacroix.

After several overtures in 1847, he received in 1849 the official commission to decorate a chapel in the Church of Saint-Sulpice. And it was only in 1861, two years before his death, that the chapel was inaugurated. This decade of ordeals, weariness, discouragement, illness, thrills, passion, and youth rediscovered amidst old age finally saw the painter's victory. But what sort of victory, exactly? This is the very question. When he began the struggle with his angel, Delacroix knew that it "[would] require much time and cause much weariness," not that this night would see dawn only after twelve years had passed.[11] While he was far from being pious, he noted that it was on October 2, 1849, Feast of the Guardian Angels, that he arrived at a definitive agreement with the curé to paint the chapel of the Holy Angels.[12] His correspondence and his diary allow us to follow the months and years of this work's bumpy and syncopated progress. With good reason Maurice Barrès entitled the magnificent essay he devoted to Delacroix *Le testament de Delacroix (Delacroix's Last Testament)*,[13] because his focus is upon the artist's final great accomplishment; yet it is worth remembering that this "testament" occupied the painter from his fifty-first to his sixty-third year, and that its agonistic amplitude flows from a mature strength, and not a decline, even a sublime one.

If, to paint Jacob, Delacroix had in some way to become Jacob, this was in no way the case at the outset. Rather, he was first like Heliodorus, to whom the other wall of the chapel is devoted: he allowed himself at several junctures to be thrown to the ground by his work, so frequently interrupted or suspended. He speaks in 1855 of "very tough work," which winds up making him "ill," and later of "very tiring work," of "galley slave labor."[14] Like Jacob remaining behind, alone, this task leads him to "the life of a cenobite," "a Carthusian's life."[15] In a striking manner, he will on several occasions go so far as to qualify this work as "infernal."[16] And in the very year in which the work was finished, Delacroix imagines himself dying at his task, in ront of an unfinished, unfinishable work. He who had said that he "threw himself recklessly" into the work, "swimming in it,"[17] writes in 1861: "Finishing requires a heart of steel . . . I believe I will die at it; it is in a moment like this that your own weakness becomes apparent, as well as the degree to which what a man calls a finished or complete work contains things that are incomplete and impossible to complete."[18] But in the end he too became Jacob, and his wounds a blessing. Barrès saw and described this well:

> He spends his time figuring a herdsman, an angel, trees, just like any painter would do, and suddenly he grasps the mysterious meaning of the old myth, he feels that this is his story, our story . . . Man does not give of himself completely unless it concerns his own destiny. As he works, this myth touches Delacroix, and impassions him as his own personal adventure. This young shepherd is he himself.[19]

This appropriation is not simply Barrès's novelistic concoction. Delacroix himself attests to it in two ways. First, at the outset of his task, he affirms that the biblical themes offer the possibility of an appropriation without equal: "Among all of the sorts of attractions that they present, religious subjects have the advantage of giving full scope to the imagination, so that each person finds in the subject what he needs to express his particular feeling."[20] The commonest and simplest is also what allows the most personal and most singular to be. The founding events of sacred history do not cease to write and prolong themselves in new existences. They have enough power and meaning that their date does not prevent them from becoming contemporaries of every present that appears. They never finish taking place, if we offer them this place that is our life. Why does Jacob matter, if we cannot become him? Why does his angel matter, if he no longer has the force to assault us? What does this combat matter, if it cannot take place this very night? And note: the scene of this struggle was not brought to Delacroix's mind solely by the commission of this chapel of the Angels—he had previously planned to paint it.[21]

This appropriation of Jacob is attested secondly by a key passage in Delacroix's *Journal,* dated January 1, 1861, the importance of which Barrès rightly highlights. He shows that, in the order of painting, it befell to Delacroix what had befallen to Jacob in the order of the spirit. Speaking of his work at the chapel of Saint-Sulpice, where he had been since that morning, he writes:

> To tell the truth, the painting badgers and torments me in a thousand ways, like the most demanding mistress . . .; what from a distance had seemed easy to surmount presents me with horrible and incessant difficulties. But how is it that this eternal combat, instead of killing me, lifts me up, and instead of discouraging me, consoles me and fills my hours when I have left it?[22]

Only the painting, he adds, gives him "the strength to surmount the bodily pains and the sufferings of the soul," but this strength gives itself only after first seizing and drawing out his own. Out of the irreparable urgency of the work to be done, this strength holds its flame higher, which consumes all other worry. In order that this hand-to-hand grappling might take place, it is necessary that Delacroix, like Jacob, first remain alone, in a solitude lovingly inhabited by his task. It is on the first day of the year 1861 that he writes the above. And he notes that, instead of making the customary visits to present his good wishes, he went to paint, just like the other days, obeying the vow to the visible, or the future of the visible, that he had made, and which binds him more than any other bond. "Celestial compensation of my supposed isolation! Brothers, fathers, relations of every degree, friends living together, all quarrel amongst themselves and hate one another using nothing but false words." These are not words of bitterness or misanthropy: they translate a separation already accomplished, of the sort that we do not determine, but which determines us.

Just as onlookers will spontaneously move apart to allow room for fighters, and others will run away out of fear of receiving a blow, an empty space inevitably forms around the one who has been seized and overtaken by the loving and terrible demand of his task, in order that he may enter into the lists. Who would be surprised at Delacroix's recourse to erotic analogies to express this grappling in which painting is his "only thought"? "I assure you," he writes to a friend, "that I run to my church with an ardor that we used to put into running to quite different places," or, in another letter, "I run there like a young man eagerly courting his mistress."[23] This isn't simply a matter of bourgeois escapades—here, concerning the work, the (for us) old-fashioned word "mistress" takes on its full stature. Every word concerning our task has a certain off-kilter quality; it is right even in its rusticity, divergent in its very precision, because the only site of acuity in this order is the work's trenchant light, which shows without adorning or comparing.

Let us enter now into the chapel of the Angels. What do we find? We are astounded, overshadowed, overwhelmed, circumvented: because of the considerable dimensions of the painting, and the impossibility of taking a step back in this chapel as narrow as it is high, the work has seen and seized us first, and its mobility has forestalled us. The gaze only begins to approach that which has already overflowed it. The disproportion is initial; forgetting suddenly all that we could have expected, we discover at our own expense that it is we who were expected. An irresistible power raises us, and knocks us down, loses us, and finds us, in dizzying whirlwinds. Nothing is complete, or comes to a close, from any angle. And yet, within what we do not manage truly to see at first, haven't we heard something, something fragile and soft amongst so much agitation, like a murmur, or an invitation, or a song? It is the burble of the water that, from far away, rushes toward us until, in the left foreground, it is appeased and calm. It is so near that it is completely natural to hear it before seeing it, the gaze having first been caught up higher, farther away, any-where else. Nothing ever happens without water. Nothing speaks without some sort of fluidity. But the water flows, washes away and is easily forgotten. This is its greatness and its secret, this is the secret of its greatness.

On the right, also in the foreground, there is another murmuring flow, but this one moves away from us. It is the foam of sheep that Jacob is sending to Esau. How strange it is that we have not taken greater notice of this deafening racket, of this caravan of noises and smells. Camels, cattle, pushing to enter into the painting and into the flux, and of which one sees only the heads; cries of shepherds; bleatings of sheep; horses, among which one has turned back, sole retrospection in this profuse and absent-minded transhumance—what echoing resonance! Just before disappearing behind the hillock we glimpse a calm sign of punctuation: a woman bearing on her head an earthenware jar, steadying it with her outstretched right arm. All of this flows, too, undulates and penetrates into what the landscape of huge trees hides from us. In the background, at the other end of the painting, some galloping horses can be seen, indicating the immensity of this caravan, which stretches out without end. By attracting us magnetically, a silence, stronger than any clamor, in which there arose only the breathing of the wrestlers, had prevented us from hearing this racket.

Delacroix allowed himself one infidelity to the letter of the biblical story that in this case opens for him a higher spiritual fidelity. He translated time into space, transposing the chronological succession into a local separation. In Genesis, it is when Jacob is alone, after having sent before him to Esau the caravan of his flocks, and ushered his entire household across the ford of the Jabbok, that the angel finally accosts him. The fight lasts all night long, and Delacroix shows it to us at the very instant at the break of day in which it draws to its close: the angel, to bring it to its end, places his hand on Jacob's thigh to wound him. According to the story, the two scenes represented—the passing of the caravan and the end of the single combat—could not be simultaneous. The caravan passed long ago, and we should be seeing Jacob and the angel one-on-one, as we do in the other works that figure this same scene.

But this translation of time and space is admirable in several respects. To begin with, the confused agitation of the caravan that moves away without any apparent suspicion of what has befallen its leader Jacob—the backward-looking horse, perhaps, is alone in sensing the event—only places into greater relief the intimate solitude of the wrestlers, figuring a separation that is an election. This combat, says Delacroix himself in the description that accompanied the invitation to the inauguration of the chapel, is "like an emblem of the trials that God sometimes sends to his elect."[24] Elevated in relation to the caravan that flows below, Jacob and the angel are only more alone, and Jacob has even turned his back to it. It is all already far-away for him. From this point on, between him and everything else, there will always be the thickness of this night. The time of daily, normal life that follows its course, and the exceptional time of mysterious trial are, thanks to the distinction of places, given to us to see in their mutual indifference and ignorance.

In other respects, Delacroix can thus figure the duration, without forgoing the decisive and crucial instant of the final wound, which precedes the benediction. The considerable distance between what seems to be the beginning of the caravan and what we see arriving and crowding in the foreground gives the work its proper temporal thickness. This train that has no end appears to measure the duration of the combat that we see just on the point of ending. And time thickens further thanks to these immense trees that overhang the wrestlers, like a canopy of centuries, and of which we see neither the edges nor the top. In this respect, the *Lutte de Jacob avec l'ange (Jacob's Wrestling With the Angel)* is radically opposed to *Héliodore chassé du temple (Heliodorus Driven From the Temple)*, which faces it in the same chapel. The *Héliodore* is indeed a work of pure event, of the suddenness of that which escapes all anticipation.

The figures' movements of surprise, of fear, and of sudden shock in front of the irruption of angels, the heavy curtain above that rises and floats as if blown by a sudden gust of wind, the leap of the horse with only one hoof on the ground, seemingly about to trample Heliodorus and land all of a sudden outside the space of the painting, the splendid angel swooping down from the sky with his rods, having just seized the terrified Heliodorus by the sleeve—an angel that flies all the more confidently because he has no wings—all of this, and many other details as well, make of this work a sudden rupture in the woof of time and the course of things. The beauty of this irruption does not appear, however, with theatricality. In his description, Delacroix rightly says that Heliodorus is "all of a sudden knocked over by a mysterious rider," and it is this "all of a sudden" that he throws before our eyes. For the agonistic embrace of Jacob and the angel, it was on the contrary necessary to depict it in its complete nocturnal extension.

Baudelaire described this combat in two sentences:

> In the foreground, on the ground, there lie the clothes and the weapons of which Jacob has disencumbered himself in order to fight hand to hand with the mysterious *man* sent by the Lord. The natural man and the supernatural man each wrestle according to his nature, Jacob leaning forward like a ram and stretching taut all of his muscles, the angel consenting complacently to the combat, calm, gentle, like a being who can conquer without any effort of his muscles, and refusing to allow anger to alter the divine form of his members.[25]

The heap of Jacob's things has about it a lively and handsome disorder. It testifies to the haste with which Jacob lightened and stripped himself to wrestle. These are also the castoffs of his life prior to this particular night, the already present trophy of the imminent defeat that will be a victory. This pile was rightly admired as a painting within the painting, a splendid still life. Nevertheless, there is nothing digressive about it. Along with the hillock that overhangs it and the powerful soaring height of the trees, the pile separates the eddy of the caravan from the combat itself. Jacob's pike and the arrows from his quiver point to the event and form part of the multiple oblique lines converging toward the wrestlers, as does the curve of the terrain. They show and, at the same time, reverberate with the main oblique line, which is Jacob's body itself, braced on his right foot, throwing in vain all his force and all his weight against the firm and upright stature of the angel with the heavy wings.

Jacob stripped his upper body naked and disarmed for combat, but has not had the time to finish the job, for at his feet there has fallen during the confrontation a dagger in its sheath and the cord that held it, serpentine and gleaming red on the grass. And in the ardor of the struggle he seems about to lose a lion skin, unexpected on him, though perhaps not under Delacroix's brush. With their lively swirls, the clothes themselves take part in the combat. In preparatory sketches, Delacroix had placed a fluttering cloth over Jacob's thigh, as if he too had a wing:[26] he ultimately kept the movement of what became a lion skin, but made it fall downwards, thus underscoring even more Jacob's impetus. At the edge of the pair the angry paw of the lion stretches, clawing at the air in vain.

The biblical account says nothing of Jacob's weapons, even if it is clear that the fight is barehanded. Delacroix is alone in introducing, with keen precision, this superabundant disarmament. To give up all defenses and weapons to enter into the fight, to confront the irresistible assailant counting on nothing more than one's own presentation, to come at him openly: such are the conditions of combats that are in truth life-and-death matters, combats in which something of ours must die, and a new life enter to dwell within us. Only the disarmed can grow in strength. To take arms, to surround oneself with defenses, is already to place oneself in a position of weakness, and at the same time to refuse the salutary intimacy of close combat. What must die in us will only truly die by not allowing itself to die, by burning up every last bit of its power, without any reserve. This is what it means to die a natural death.

Baudelaire stresses the angel's calm. Certain sketches show it troubled, unbalanced by Jacob, which conforms more closely to the narrative account, while one among them goes so far as to depict the angel with a terrible and fierce expression.[27] In the finished work, the angel's situation is not without complexity. On the one hand, he seems to be the assaulted more than the assailant, and he is backed up against the bank of the Jabbok, as if he had been pushed that far by Jacob's power. On the other hand, details such as the serenity of his handsome face crowned by blond locks, and the firm and already blessing gaze he places upon Jacob, against whom his powerful wings, unmoved by the least quiver, form a definitive counterweight, make of him this unshakeable wall against which human effort will vainly break. The certain and precise wound that his right hand inflicts upon Jacob's thigh seems to cost him nothing.

The meditative light of dawn falls upon these conflicting bodies, upon the vigorous back of Jacob, and on their interlocked hands, raised above them, as if they were arm wrestling. All the violence of the fight is manifested there, as is too the balance of forces that the other hand of the angel will break with a simple movement. Their intertwining renders intimacy adverse and adversity intimate. One day a painter eventually has to discharge himself of his praise of hands. He has to elevate them above all things, like an original explosion of pure energy. What would we see without hands? There is a world only through them. One of the sketches at Vienna indicates by a quick, light touch the body and the face of the wrestlers, but lingers firmly and powerfully on the cupola of united hands and their forearms.[28] In other sketches, they are a maelstrom of force in which one can no longer distinguish one from the other. Let us leave these hands silently vibrating in the imminence of the word. The imminence of a blessing is already a blessing. It is a violent imminence. The Holy Scripture says that "the Kingdom of heaven has suffered violence" and that "the violent take it by force."[29] This violence must not be appeased.

NOTES

1. Plutarch, *Lives, Pyrrhus*, XXI, vol. IX: 417 [translation modified].

2. Rilke, "Der Schauende," *Das Buch der Bilder (The Book of Images)*, II, 2: 211, 213.

3. Gen. 32:25–29, Jerusalem Bible [translation modified].

4. Philo, *De somniis*, I:129; tran. Colson and Whitaker, *Philo*, 5:367 [translation slightly modified].

5. Philo, *De somniis*, I:130; tran. Colson and Whitaker, *Philo*, 5:367.

6. Philo, *De somniis*, I:131; tran. Colson and Whitaker, *Philo*, 5:369 [translation modified].

7. Philo, *De praemiis et poenis*, 48; tran. Colson, *Philo*, 8:341.

8. Justin Martyr, *Dialogue With Tryphon*, 125–26.

9. François de Sales, *Œuvres*, t. XIII (Annecy: J. Niérat, et al., 1904), Letter 308.

10. Chardon, *La croix de Jésus*, III:27 (1647; republished 1937), 526–27.

11. The monumental work of Maurice Sérullaz, *Les peintures murales de Delacroix*, usefully gathers (149–82) all the documents relating to the genesis of the work. Here, see 151.

12. Ibid., 152.

13. Barrès, *Le mystère en pleine lumière*, 93–116.

14. Sérullaz, *Les peintures murales*, 155, 163.

15. Ibid., 157, 163.

16. Ibid., 158, 163.

17. Ibid., 158–59.

18. Ibid., 163.

19. Barrès, *Le mystère*, 104.

20. Sérullaz, *Les peintures murales*, 154.

21. Spector, *The Murals of Eugène Delacroix*, 108.

22. Delacroix, *Journal* (Paris: Plon, 1980), 796.

23. Sérullaz, *Les peintures murales*, 162–63.

24. Ibid., 165.
25. Baudelaire, *Œuvres complètes*, 1109.
26. Spector, *Murals*, 57.
27. Ibid., 56.
28. Ibid., 57.
29. Matt. 11:12.

Silence in Painting

WHEN WE LOOK at a picture, we do not suddenly become one big eye, for we have two eyes that make a single gaze, which the whole body brings to bear upon that which presents itself, and upon that in front of which the gaze, too, presents itself. One in two: just as we have two hands for a single grasp, and two ears for a single act of listening, but one voice to utter everything, this lively gaze serves as the van for our entire body. It is not with one's eyes but rather with all one's being that one looks upon a picture. In a manner exactly opposite to the other sensory faculties, the wake of our gaze precedes our movements, and precedes them only when it itself moves. In order to look, it is necessary to draw near, to back away, to draw near and to back away again, and to be quiet and to stay still, which is for us yet another action.

Silence in painting seems at first to be a vain object for consideration because redundant or tautological. Isn't it obvious that painting neither speaks nor sings? If Lessing among others could contest the ancient saying of Simonides, as reported by Plutarch, according to which painting is mute poetry, and poetry a speaking painting, objections of this sort aimed only at the analogy between painting and poetry and did not claim that painting is essentially silent.[1] But what exactly is this silence? For what, precisely, in or about us, is it silence?

Aristotle could say that "hearing is [the sense] of sound and of silence, the one audible, the other inaudible."[2] Thus, there is silence only for listening. A deaf person does not live in a silent world, but rather a world where the difference between the sonorous and the insonorous does not exist, a world that is deprived of sound, but also of silence. To say that painting is silent is to say that we not only see it, but that we listen to it as well. Crossing hearing and seeing Paul Claudel shed light on this issue with great rigor in the formula that serves as the title to his book on painting and informs the title of this book, as well: *The Eye Listens (L'œil écoute)*.[3] We listen to pictures just as we listen to anything, by making ourselves silent, by entering into the active silence of attention. It is with *our* silence that we listen to the silence in painting: two antiphonic silences, two silences that respond to one another, give one another a fresh start, and in a certain sense embrace one another. True silence is never alone. And silence in painting, when it is truly silent, *calls* forth our silence, too: we can be speaking with a friend in a museum or gallery, when all of a sudden a picture imposes silence upon us.

And yet, however good this question may be, it seems to come up short; for if painting is silent in its essence, any picture would be silent insofar as it is a plastic work, and thus there would be nothing to differentiate one picture's silence from that of another picture, and thus nothing to add to these general preliminary remarks. But is it certain that this "great lesson of silence that painters suspend around us," spoken of by a Japanese man in *The Satin Slipper*,[4] is given with the same authority by all painters? The essential silence of painting is a communicative, radiant, and cordial silence, which invites us to live within it. It cannot be reduced to a silence of privation, to the obviously and trivially insonorous character of a picture. Empirical works of art do not equally or with the same assuredness accomplish the particular art's essence. They can forget or lose the silence toward which they tend, and which is their true origin only when it is also their endpoint, destination, or mission. There are garrulous, speechifying, and deafening paintings, and others that are intensely silent, but with a silence that certainly tells itself in several ways, in death or in life, in presence or in absence, in anguish or in prayer. Despite first appearances, the silence *of* painting and the silence *in* painting present a rich internal differentiation, and the grain of their phenomenality is as fine as it is varied.

To begin with, there is a dimension of pictorial silence, or of its absence that belongs to what makes the image in painting, which is to say, there is an iconographic silence: what is given to us to see can be silent, or not, and of various silences. A still life by Chardin is silent in a different way from the battles of Alexander according to Charles Le Brun, where convulsed bodies and panic-stricken horses fall upon one another with extreme violence in inhuman formats that spill beyond our gaze and our presence. The quality of the silence differs by the nature of the scene as much as by the manner of painting. And thus there is another silence as well, that of the pictorial project as such, for a still life by Chardin is silent as well with regard to another, anterior kind of still life, such as the "vanities." These, according to a highly subtle symbolism laden with history, teach us without words what could also be told by words, and once was: for instance, that all flesh is doomed to corruption, that its fascinating charm is ephemeral, that the worm is already in the fruit, and that the perfection of precious objects, in which human talent glitters, will not deliver us from death. They not only show, but illustrate, as well. In contrast, Chardin, far from any taste for allegory and torn from all illustration, in a sense throws us into the simple mystery of the common things with which we deal every day, without seeing them: a knife, a mug, a pitcher. The mystery here is that of our very corporal existence in the world. A silent painting is also an *interrogative* painting. It does not deliver a message that, in advance, it knows that it knows, a message it would own. Rather, it delivers us over to the admiration of visible things, to this learned ignorance that fills us with wonder.

It is this sort of silence that Georges Bataille, in his book on Manet, describes as having been introduced by Manet:

a silence *of* painting itself. "The various paintings since Manet's time are the various possibilities encountered within this new region, where silence reigns profoundly,"[5] and for him this "great silence,"[6] "this passion to reduce to silence—in a sort of operation—that of which the natural movement is to speak,"[7] coincides with the birth of modernity in painting, and also with painting's access to its proper essence. These theses can certainly be contested, as can the attribution to Manet of the paternity of this "great silence," but the question posed cannot be sidestepped. The interrogation of silence in painting, which at first appeared tautological, becomes henceforth of such richness that it is difficult to master and to articulate.

To attempt to clear a path, it is just as well to go straight to the point, which is to say, as always, paradoxically, by meditating upon *silent music.* What could be more silent, indeed, than a silent music, an unheard or insonorous music? Silent music is the very music of silence, silence as music. From the very fact of its being music, it gives a singular density to silence. If we were to look upon musicians playing through a pane of glass so thick that it prevented us from hearing what they were playing, this would not be a music of silence, but rather a forbidden music, a frustrating music that would exasperate our desire to hear. But all of the songs of angels or of men, all of the pictorial concerts, performed solo or by groups, which traverse the many centuries of painting, give us silence to hear. We are deprived of nothing; on the contrary, we are filled. From the painting of Pompeii, with its strolling musicians and its admirable Pan encircled by nymphs, to the guitars and mandolins of Braque and of Picasso, painting is peopled by a crowd of musicians, and abounds in thousands of musical instruments. They render silence more present and more vibrant than in the vain allegories of silence, where we see someone placing a finger to his lips to symbolize or signify it. Keats interrogated this silent music in an unforgettable way in his "Ode on a Grecian Urn," which, beyond meditation on the work of art—the urn and its friezes—means as well to draw the lesson of art in general. Who better, then, than Keats to introduce silent music?

Although the ode is "on" a Greek urn, and not "to" it, the poem begins with a familiar "thou," a word addressed to the work being contemplated: "Thou still unravish'd bride of quietness,/Thou foster-child of silence and slow time."[8] The dimensions of silence, of slowness, and of quietness are no longer only those in which the urn sits; they belong to it, they have become a part of its very existence by forming with it personal, intimate relations.[9] The bride of quietness can only be virginal, and she who is nourished by silence and slow time can only herself radiate silence and patience. We learn *who* the urn is, and *how* she lives, since from the outset she is shown to us as living, before we know *what* she is and what appears upon her. All the same, the description in the first stanza of the first scene represented is wholly interrogative, which will not be the case in the second and third stanzas. To address a visible work is to see while listening to, or to listen to while seeing, its silence. Only this listening can give the poet speech: he does not take speech, he receives it.

He receives it in an act of listening to a silence that is worthy of obedience *(audire, obaudire)*, for he knows from the beginning the unevenness between what he sees and what he says: "who canst thus express/A flowery tale more sweetly than our rhyme":[10] who, indeed, if not the urn itself upon which he gazes? The poet in turn is also nourished by the silence of the urn. But the first scene among the friezes is an orgiastic one[11] in which men, or gods, pursue maidens in an atmosphere of frenzy and musical trance: "What pipes and timbrels? What wild ecstasy?"[12] So goes the final verse of the first stanza. And at this point of violence and suspense, where the hurried and almost panting questions of the poet mimic the "mad pursuit" itself, the second stanza intervenes, with its admirable verses, bringing us into another, more peaceful scene, where a young man has music played for the one he is courting: "Heard melodies are sweet, but those unheard/ Are sweeter; therefore, ye soft pipes, play on;/Not to the sensual ear, but, more endear'd,/Pipe to the spirit ditties of no tone."[13]

Silence here forms a superior music, and, as one of Keats's commentators says, "not to hear is to hear most essentially."[14] At issue in this silent music is not an oxymoron but, rather, the essence of music. This music avoids any alteration, and becomes an ever vibrant music, because "for ever new," as the third stanza says, thus evoking the "happy melodist, unwearied,/For ever piping songs for ever new."[15] This music that has been interrupted and immobilized by the image, like the gesture of the lover that will never touch the beloved, becomes for Keats a perennial and uninterrupted music, the music of silence itself, music prior to and following the sounds that resonate.

It is worth pondering the fact that, when Stéphane Mallarmé evokes the patroness of musicians, Saint Cecilia, he too will bring forth an image of the music of silence. Initially, the poem held the parenthetical subtitle "ancient song and image."[16] The title itself teaches how to be silent because it became simply and anonymously "Sainte," after having been "Sainte Cécile Playing on the Wing of a Cherubim." The poem enacts in itself the music it describes. It ends, or opens out, with the movement of the "délicate phalange"

> Du doigt que, sans le vieux santal
> Ni le vieux livre, elle balance
> Sur le plumage instrumental
> Musicienne du silence.
>
> . . . the delicate fingertip
> Which, without the old, worn missal
> Or sandalwood, she balances
> On the plumage instrumental,
> Musician of silence.

The diaeresis in the last verse sings a music that is itself perennial, on an instrument that is only visible, barely visible.

As for John Keats, this listening that speaks of and sees "unheard melodies" ends with the ode itself, by making itself a listening to the *speaking* silence of the urn: that which was addressed itself comes around, through patience, to address us, with the famous final verses, pronounced by the work of art:[17] "Beauty is truth, truth beauty,—that is all/Ye know on earth, and all ye need to know."[18] Rilke, with a comparable movement, makes his poem "Archaic Torso of Apollo" end with "You must change your life," which can hardly be understood otherwise than coming from the work contemplated by the poet. There is here a perfect mutuality in the contemplation: that which made us speak is that by which we will let ourselves say something. And that which one allows oneself to say by dint of listening always has, in its very gentleness, an imperious tone. The urn speaks through the mouth of the poet: is this indeed, as one commentator states, "his supreme gift to the urn," which "could speak only by its pictures," or is it not rather the supreme and ultimate gift of the urn itself?[19]

When there is music present, the silence of the work of plastic art thus becomes a musical silence, which is given to us to hear. In his book on the Renaissance, Walter Pater wrote many profound remarks on the subject: "In the school of Giorgione, the perfect moments of music itself, the making or hearing of music, song, or its accompaniment, are themselves prominent as subjects. On that background of the silence of Venice, so impressive to the modern visitor, the world of Italian music was then forming."[20] And Pater nicely evokes examples of the presence of music in the painting of the period before writing this powerful sentence: "In these then, the favourite incidents of Giorgione's school, music or the musical intervals in our existence, life itself is conceived as a sort of listening—listening to music, to the reading of Brunello's novels, to the sound of water, to time as it flies."[21] It is just such a listening, a listening that for us is listening to silence, that painting gives to us according to various possibilities.

Thus does a Dutch painting from the beginning of the seventeenth century, of uncertain attribution, suggest, as H. Diane Russell notes, that *ut pictura musica*, and not only *ut pictura poesis*.[22] We see a painter, seated before a landscape finished yet still on his easel, playing the lute, having put aside his palette and his brushes, which appear in the foreground. The painting and the painter musician look at us according to two fraternal melodies. Music and painting are here expressly associated. The one attests the dignity of the other. The ironic chiasmus of such a praise of painting by association with music exists in another Dutch painting of the same period: the *Self Portrait* by Judith Leyster.[23] The painter, clothed elaborately and enlivened by a mischievous smile, stands, palette in hand, before a picture showing a mirthful village fiddler. His bow answers to the brush that she holds in her hand. His humor has nothing in common with the solemnity of the other canvas, stamped with seriousness. With regard to the latter, Russell recalls a scene from the life of Barocci, who called "painting 'music,' as, for instance, when questioned one time by Duke Guidobaldo, Barocci referred to what he was doing as making music, pointing out the picture he was painting."[24] In the same way an otologist reports that, one day, a painter came for a consultation, confiding to him, "I have come to see you because I no longer hear the colors."[25]

Of course, all of this raises the issue of intersensoriality and the Baudelairean "correspondences" that may ground a relationship between music and painting more than it addresses the question of silence. Nevertheless it is not immaterial that the Dutch painter represents herself in front of a landscape painting. The landscape painting is indeed one of the important sites of silence in painting. When it emerges as a genre, when landscape ceases to be the décor or the background of a story or an event, it delivers to our presence the frightening or joyful silence of nature. What an ancestral, majestic, affirming silence in the great trees of Claude Lorrain! Every human voice, indeed all human existence seems as if it could be overwhelmed! And yet this silence is hospitable, for Claude within this lofty jewel-case for listening likes to make peasants dance, as in his *Fête villageoise* in the Louvre. A *Pastoral Landscape with Piping Shepherd*,[26] if it lacks the same perfection, nevertheless possesses a grace all its own.

In the foreground, seated on an immense trunk of a felled tree, a young shepherd, barefoot and wearing a red hat that seems to anticipate Corot, plays the flute. Above him, on the left, there stand some intermingled trees for which the space of the picture is insufficient. Sunlight outlines the leaves of some among them, while others keep their shadowy reserve. Some cattle move off; one beast stays, listening. From the other side of an inlet of the sea glimpsed behind the young man there rises a bare, grassy promontory where a road winds toward a shelter, and continues its undulations farther on again toward other shelters. In the distance a hazy mountain fades away, blessed by the light. The entire work rests upon the tension between the ideal splendor of the landscape, ample, open in every way, and the tenuousness of the sound of the flute. This latter, so fragile and so high-pitched, can only vanish and become lost without having reached any of these distances offered to our view. The melody's evanescence is like the signature of the great silence of nature: it is what makes us truly hear it. This work is in this manner more silent than if it were deprived of music. The young man's solitude, playing only for himself, like a dreamer, reinforces it all the more.

The flute in Thomas Eakins's *Arcadia* is completely different.[27] While Eakins is especially known as a painter of modern life, he indulges here in a reverie on ancient images. Upon grass that seems to have lost all materiality, flowing with softness rather than being a veritable ground, there are three figures. A naked young man, standing, seen in profile, plays the double flute in the direction of two children lying on the ground, one upon a white sheet and the other directly upon the grass. They look toward him, and one of the two plays the panpipes. The meadow upon which they happen to be is encircled with trees and shrubs, which isolate them in a room of greenery. The silence revealed by the music is a silence of intimacy: it is like an interior scene outside. The sound does not go forth to lose itself in the distance, because the almost cottony vegetation underscores the sharpness of bodies and melodies. The point here is not to listen to the silence of nature but rather to show Nature herself listening, discrete, unobtrusive— nature that has become all hearing, nothing more than a sensual and unreal decor for man. Yet it is nature that both listens and sings through the wood of the flute and the reeds of the panpipes, and is reinforced by the nudity of the body, torn from any sign of history and any determined sociality.

More forceful and more monumental is the silent music of Picasso's admirable *Flûte de Pan*.[28] Against a background of a sea rising high toward the sky, in a completely square architecture, are two men, one seated, the other standing, like a new version of Apollo and Marsyas. One plays the panpipes, the other listens to him with the absent gaze that denotes attention. Their bodies, outlined by a simple and pure line that the shadows and the background render even more marked, are powerfully volumetric. They are not so much sculptural as architectural. Their arms and legs have the solidity of columns. Feet and hands of impossible proportions, fitting for these giants, repeat and take up again the motif of the panpipes. Ancient authors had compared the human body to a musical instrument, whether cithara or flute,[29] but here, in this compact space, with these smooth bodies from which all asperity and all inequality have been effaced, it is not so much breath, which seems to be suspended in these two men and in the landscape, that makes of man an instrument, as the form of the body, for a silent music. The two bodies occupy, in height and in width, the entire space of the picture; there is space only for them, which gives the painting its hieratism.

Only its immobility preserves us from suffocation. Gilded and curved liked fruits, these bodies nevertheless have nothing sensual about them: there is something Pythagorean in this so perfectly ordered and totally definitive world. Our gaze enters into an elsewhere where it truly has no place, where it is not welcomed, where everything in a sense pushes it away massively: the wall of the sea, the equilibrium of the blue-black sky, the architecture of these autarkic bodies, the perspective that deflects us. The absent gaze of one of the two men, and the lowered gaze of the other have left us only a powerful silence to encounter, which the flute, again, makes us hear.

This musical silence inhabiting so many paintings down through the centuries incarnates, in its very paradox, veritable silence even more than any explicit invitation to quiet oneself, such as the placing of a raised index finger against the lips. The gesture is already present in ancient art: it is the gesture of the Egyptian god Harpocrate, which is to say Horus as a child. Plutarch evokes him thus, in his *Isis and Osiris:* "For this reason he keeps his finger on his lips in token of restrained speech and silence."[30] A scholarly editor of the treatise reports that, at its origin, the representation was that of a child sucking his finger, and not of an invitation to keep quiet about the divine secrets.[31] The *Cupidon assis* by the sculptor Falconet, charming perhaps, but more certainly just pretty, holds a finger up to his lips, while with the other hand he prepares to draw an arrow from his quiver, which, as Michael Levey notes,[32] gives an ambiguity to his gesture (complicity, or threat?): he at least has the merit of acknowledging himself anecdotal and decorative. This is not the case with the nineteenth-century sculptor Préault's *Silence,* which, despite its pompous stiffness, had its moment of glory when Michelet wrote of it as "That truly terrible work, whose impression the heart can hardly bear, and which looks to have been cut with the great chisel of death."[33] This heavy piece, in which an old, emaciated woman seals her lips with a finger, replaces silence with the sign of silence. But the sign of silence is not itself silent; on the contrary, it chatters and elicits chatter, hence its success. Romantic imaginations were no doubt struck by the fact that this work was destined for a funerary monument at Père-Lachaise cemetery. The sign of silence quickly becomes insignificant, as in the works of Fernand Khnopff or other *symbolistes,* where it is repeated on young and beautiful diaphanous women, a decision that, in rendering the gesture provocative, ballasts it with little meaning. All of this simply elicits boredom. Let us leave these noisy frivolities to find a more thoroughgoing silence.

In painting there is the music one plays, the pastoral or intimate concerts, and all of the "unheard melodies" that Keats called "sweeter," but there is also the music that one does not play, that one no longer or does not yet play, in other words the still life with musical instruments. The musical instrument placed, laid down, abandoned, has a presence all its own. Like a mind asleep, which no longer thinks anything, it is the virtuality of all melodies without playing any of them. It is the very realm of sound, the royalty of the sonorous, not captive of silence as if it were in exile, but delivered up to silence where it exerts its plenitude before any choice. The mother of all sounds does not herself resonate, and yet she is a musician.

This is what Stéphane Mallarmé says in a sonnet about a dreamed-of mandora (a *"mandore,"* named thus by Diderot himself, holds a place of honor, though it is not seen in its potbellied profile, in Chardin's *Les attributs de la musique*):[34]

> Tristement dort une mandore
> Au creux néant musicien
>
> Sadly sleeps a mandolin,
> The hollow core's musician[35]

There is something oriental, and almost Taoist, in this musical primacy of the void, but the "Tristement dort" also evokes with precision the fleshly presence, in dereliction, of the instrument lying prone, without any hand holding it or making it resonate and thereby waking it from the spell that has struck it down. This is no longer Taoist, and serves all the more to put painting into play. Braque will remember this. But well before anyone painted silent mandoras, there existed a meditation upon the forsaken instrument and the music that goes without instruments, a music that goes without precisely because it has truly become music, and truly become silent: the meditation of the philosopher Plotinus at the end of his treatise *On Happiness.*

Plotinus's goal is to describe the life of the wise man, and the relation he has with his body. The latter has for Plotinus its role and its price, but in the end the wise man will come to forsake it. And Plotinus, who has a musical vision of life and of the act of life, concludes his treatise with a rigorously grounded analogy. The wise man "will care for his body and will support it, as long as possible, just as will a musician his lyre, just as long as he can make use of it; and if he no longer can, either he will exchange it for another" (a possibility obviously excluded in this case, because Plotinus here is describing a single incarnated life, and not the transmigration of souls),

> or he will give up the use of lyres, and will cease the activities involving the lyre, having henceforth another work to do without the lyre: he will look upon it lying next to him with indifference, he who now sings without instruments. And yet it was not without good reason that in the beginning the instrument was given to him. For he frequently made good use of it.[36]

Two silences are opposed here: the silence of the instrument that is the body (but which we should note is a lyre that the soul makes use of to sing the song that is its own, which has nothing pejorative about it); and the silence of a higher music, into which the soul alone advances. Silence of the means, of that which will have been a precious, but only provisionary, moment of music, and silence of an end that is still a path, the journey of the soul toward the first principle. For this song that the soul sings without instruments is an unheard melody, a song completely insonorous, heard by no ear: the song of the soul. What do we see when we see a forsaken instrument? That there isn't any more music, that it's all over with music? Or that the instrument was forsaken for the sake of another music, even purer and higher? For Plotinus, the lyre one no longer uses is not thrown away nor broken, it is still near, even if one looks at it henceforth without seeing it. Raphael's *Saint Cecilia* holds herself in a position that is at the same time both similar and different. Holding in her hand a portable organ, she listens, her head turned toward the sky, to "the choir of angels whose vocal concert," writes Daniel Arasse, "no longer needs instrumental mediation,"[37] but which, we must add, still needs the mediation of the parts from which they read. Even the angels need an antiphonary. "Placed above broken or worn out instruments that are scattered on the ground like symbols of profane and terrestrial music," continues Arasse, this organ "figures the instrument with which Cecilia translated the interior and spiritual music of which she had the divine revelation." Thus, a double forsaking. But Saint Cecilia does not let go of her organ, even if she holds it with the negligence that Plotinus attributed to the gaze of the wise man upon his lyre.

Painting, which remains in an indefectible attachment to what can be sensed, has that chance, that near-grace— all grace is near-grace, otherwise it would take hold of itself and would no longer be grace—to be able to make us hear this song without instruments by showing us the instruments themselves, for this song without instruments thus becomes that of the instruments themselves, insofar as it is rendered visible. There is no longer any alternative between visible and invisible, audible and inaudible. Such at least is the hypothesis, which now must be verified.

It can certainly happen that the forsaken instrument no longer has any song, and symbolizes the pure and simple abandonment of music. This is clearly the case in the shameless and provocative painting of Caravaggio, *Amor vincit omnia,* in which a lute, a violin, a bow, and a score lay upon the ground amidst other objects metonymic of their arts or evocative of the sciences and of various possibilities in life, such as armor for military glory, which have been defeated by a love that has nothing spiritual about it.[38] In *The Lute Player,* an earlier canvas that is also openly erotic, Caravaggio had painted these same instruments, the lute in the hands of the young man, and the violin placed in front of him on the table.[39] Love sang its madrigal. But, in *Amor vincit omnia,* love is no longer a musician, and the instruments lie as if dead. However remarkably summoned they may be, they have no value in themselves, but are only symbolic of musical culture, with the order and the harmony that it carries within it, defeated by the unbridled violence of passion and seduction.

In the Caravaggian tradition, the seventeenth-century Bergamese painter Evaristo Baschenis left an entire series of wonderful still lifes with musical instruments. Why, like certain art historians,[40] transform into narrative something whose beauty lies precisely in its not telling anything, by imagining that we are present after a concert, and that the musicians have set down their instruments? A musician takes more care of his instrument, especially one as precious as those of Baschenis. Their improbable disorder is a plastic composition that translates their abolished music into a visible polyphony. Charles Sterling cannot keep himself from speaking of them in musical terms: "He drew a wonderful plastic music from viols and lutes. Their rounded, smooth, or grooved bodies, their taut necks and their curved scrolls answer one another through the half light with echoes of arabesques and silky gleams."[41] Baschenis likes to represent stringed instruments turned over on their tops to allow the light to caress their wood. A ribbon is sometimes tied to the lutes. This music of silence has nothing

melancholic about it, like that evoked later by Georges
Rodenbach, in his *Règne du silence* ("Reign of Silence"):

> Il flotte une musique éteinte en de certaines
> Chambres, une musique aux tristesses lointaines
> Qui s'apparie à la couleur des meubles vieux . . .
> Musique d'ariette en dentelle et fumée,
> Ariette d'antan qu'on aurait exhumée,
> Informulée encore, et qu'on cherche des yeux.

> A faint music floats in certain
> Rooms, a music of far away sadness
> Which matches the color of old furniture . . .
> The music of an arietta in lace and in smoke,
> An arietta of long ago, recently exhumed,
> Still unformulated, sought out by sight.[42]

This sort of *fin-de-siècle* spleen is foreign to Baschenis.
His is a festive music, of jubilatory splendor. It is full of
affirmation. And, though Baschenis was a priest, it is also
assuredly a profane music. It is rare to hear a music so
warm and roborative.

And yet . . . A disquiet sometimes troubles this festivity.
In the still life at Brussels and the one at Milan, there
appear two fruits: in the former both fruits lie upon a guitar, and in the latter one fruit lies upon a thick book that is
marked with a bookmark, while a second sits upon a small
box. Certainly, their function is also plastic, and their sensual rotundity responds to that of the lute case. But their
incongruous situation in the painting underlines also their
symbolic function. The fruit whose pretty color soon
becomes spotted and speckled, and whose flavor is destined to become tainted quickly, is a paraph of these still
lifes that are the vanities. The fruits fulfill the function of
Memento mori. The music too will end. Such would be the
traditional iconographic interpretation. Nevertheless must
not prevent us from seeing. From seeing, notably,
that the mode of being of a fruit and that of a musical
instrument are not the same. And also from seeing that the
temporality of a fruit and that of music are not the same.

Aristotle remarks in his *Physic* hat a bed, insofar as it is a work of human art, has absolut y no natural tendency to change: as bed, it is torn from mutability. Of course, it will end up falling apart or its wood will decompose, but it is precisely the wood that decomposes, and not the bed.[43] Rotten wood is still wood, but a bed that has fallen in is no longer a bed. How does his relate to the works of Baschenis? The wood that makes the instruments is no longer that of a tree: it has been worked, rounded, polished, varnished, it is kept up with care; and certain instruments can last for centuries, longer than the tree from which their wood was taken. Music is not eternal, but the instrument, as Hegel will reflect, certainly lasts longer than men. The lutemaker will perish well before his lute. This is evident in this profusion of learnedly geometrical forms, fully penetrated by thought. The seemingly automatic deciphering of symbols by iconography should not blind us to the things themselves, whose glory and increase painting also teaches us to see. Thus the still lifes of Baschenis are definitely joyful. The fruit will rot, but the music will be able to make itself heard again: it is *written*, we see the scores next to the instruments, it can be played an indefinite number of times. Its time is not of the same order as that of fruit. From its silent jewel-case of writing, from the ductile silence of durable instruments, it will always be possible to make it sound again. That music is not what saves us is another affair. Who would ever imagine it could, if he at least knows what the words "to save" mean?

In the next century, Chardin too (albeit in the commissioned works) will paint musical instruments. The *Attributs de la musique* is his most accomplished work in this vein.[44] It drew, along with the works accompanying it, the admiration of Diderot, who remarks upon its eloquent silence: "Here you are again, then, great magician, with your mute compositions! May they speak eloquently to the artist!"[45] But the same Diderot, who enumerates the instruments represented by Chardin, grants no importance whatsoever to what the painting may say about music, and, amazed by what he considers the conjuring power of the artist, says rather strangely with regard to this peaceful and joyful painting: "If a harmful animated being, a serpent, was painted so accurately, it would frighten."[46] Things are completely the opposite for Francis Ponge, who, in his text *De la nature morte et de Chardin*, takes his bearings and his starting point from this precise canvas, which he names *La bougie (The Candle)*.[47] If he evokes the "silence" of Chardin,[48] understood as "a pure and simple abstention from themes imposed by the ideology of the time," he sees clearly that this silence is completely musical. And Ponge speaks of the "chamber music" of Chardin, comparing him to the musician Rameau. But it is notable that, while he organizes the entire beginning of his text around music and listening ("I listen to / The world like a symphony"), Ponge makes only the mute candle sing and the extinguished candle glow, which is to say, the only thing in the painting, apart from the books and scores, which is not a musical instrument.

It is in the candle that Ponge, without ever naming the trumpet, nor the mandora, nor the flute, nor the violin, collects the songs of these instruments, in order finally to listen to the candle's silence:

I put forth, for instance, *La Bougie* as a solo—
What does it have to say?
—Go on, I'm listening.
And so it expresses itself;
It can express itself according to all the variations,
The "Cadenzas"
Which please it. . . .
It puts on airs, shows off, perhaps with a bit of exaggeration,
Then returns into the shadows—and I follow it with my eyes:
It is then that its murmur touches me the most.[49]

Of what nature is the silent music in this canvas by Chardin? It is jubilatory and almost exclamatory, and perhaps this painting is one of the least silent of Chardin's works. The polyphony of the multiple reds—the music stand, the musette's cover, the book edges, etc.—gives it a strong resonance, as does the contrast between the stringed instruments, most of which are lying down, and the wind instruments, most of which are standing upright, with the extremities opposed, to produce a glorious explosion of sound. The composition is completely different from that in the works of Baschenis, and holds less in secret, though it is just as sure.

The function of musical instruments in the allegorical tradition of still lifes evoking the five senses is quite different. The instrument offers no silent song, but is simply metonymic of music in general, which itself reflects back on the sense of hearing. Such is the case in a work by Pierre Subleyras.[50] It constitutes the exact inverse of Caravaggio's *Amor vincit omnia,* as Sterling's analysis shows.[51] The reduction of a famous statue of Saint Suzanne, who over- turned the idols, "points out with a reproachful finger both a mutilated ancient statue . . . and a *fiasco* along with a glass of wine: these are the symbols of material life, away from which she turns in order to look at the symbols of the life of the spirit represented by the arts," a violin, some scores, and also, of course, a palette with brushes. . . . Doubtless, too much said.

Silent music made a prodigious resurgence in the Cubist era with Picasso, Braque, and Juan Gris. It may be that there has never been a moment in the history of painting in which so many canvases were so expressly musical and at the same time so profoundly silent. There are certainly scenes in which music is played: numerous men and women with guitars or clarinets by Picasso or Braque in the second decade of the century, up to the *Trois musiciens masqués* by Picasso in 1921; but even more frequent are the still lifes with musical instruments. One could say of these years what Walter Pater said of the era of Giorgione, even though it is assuredly another kind of music, another kind of listening, and another kind of painting that is at issue. Not without some emphasis, Guillaume Apollinaire said of

Braque in 1908: "A colored lyricism, the examples of which are all too rare, fills him with a harmonious enthusiasm, and his musical instruments are made to sound by Saint Cecilia herself."[52] And Juan Gris asserted that Braque had found a new Madonna in the guitar.[53] But, if the guitar became in some way emblematic in Cubism, it is far from being the only instrument present there: clarinets, pianos, violins, flutes, and mandolins appear too. And outside of painting and *papiers collés*, Picasso, in 1912 and after, also made guitars out of cardboard, as well as a clarinet and a mandolin. The "unheard melodies" are not the prerogative of earlier painting.

What a powerful silence there is in the instruments of Braque! Does the very word instrument still fit here? They no longer serve to play music, but are the silent song of music itself. And the visible guitars certainly have another sonority than those that we can hear played. The latter have a thin, faded, timid sound, while the visible guitar has full and sensual curves, an ample sound, a powerful architectonics that Cubism is pleased to split up and recombine, according to an austere, serious game. Witness *La Mandore* of 1910,[54] where one cannot fail to hear an homage to Mallarmé, given the rarity of the term and the archaic character of the instrument: the *"creux néant musicien"* has in a sense exploded and delivered its sonority in a counterpoint of Cézannean obliques. Even more, consider *Le concert* of 1937, which, while it carries its title on its canvas, in capital letters, is a concert with one single instrument (again, the guitar), and without instrumentalists.[55]

On a table covered with a cloth there figures a guitar, a half-rolled-up paper upon which one reads, backwards and in capital letters, the word "Etude," lacking, like "Concert," its final letter, a bunch of black grapes that extend the guitar ("Each atom of silence / Is the chance of a ripe fruit" says Paul Valéry in *Palme*), a dish containing undetermined, perfectly circular fruits, and a pitcher, half in shadow and half in light, with a disproportionate handle, and whose shape responds to that of the guitar. What we have, then, is a still life with guitar. Commentators recall opportunely one of the meanings that Littré gives for the word "concert": "harmony of several voices or of several instruments." But this harmony is here completely silent. And the guitar alone, thanks to which this silence becomes concerted, emits no sonority whatsoever. We understand how it could have been written that "Braque is the archetype of the musical painter."[56] But it is clearly the music of silence that we are talking about.

Between the solitary instrument and the instrument that one plays, there is the instrument that one holds in one's hands without playing it. At the end of his life, Corot on several occasions painted his studio. A woman always appears, in various costumes and various postures, but always in front of a painting, framed or without a frame, on an easel, and which is always a landscape, which should not surprise us. Sometimes she examines the canvas with attention, sometimes she seems lost in a daydream, sometimes she looks toward the viewer, but most of the time she holds a mandolin. She has often been seen as Corot's muse of painting, and it is noteworthy that this muse is a musician. But the music is held in suspense, we have passed from heard melodies to the unheard melodies of the painting itself. The silence of the studio, the silence of the pictorial work is expressly shown as a musical silence.

Now let us turn to a completely different silent music that is given to us to hear and to see, an angelic music, to which only Saint Francis of Assisi was permitted to listen during a miraculous episode of his life, and which painting, wishing to evoke it (something it does often), shows to all—to all those who cannot and would not be able to perceive it. The story of this miracle is reported, with several variants, in the various biographies of the saint. Saint Francis was staying at Rieti, reports the *Vita secunda* of Thomas of Celano, and, finding himself sick (in the eyes) and afflicted, he desired to hear music in order to be comforted.[57] A friar

who had been a musician in the world avoided responding
to Saint Francis's wish, out of fear that this exercise might
appear too frivolous and irreligious. But the following
night, when Saint Francis was on his bed, "a cithara suddenly made heard a marvelous sound and spun a delight-
ful melody. No one was seen, but one could follow the
comings and goings of the citharist by the sound. The
sweet song was such a pleasure for the saint yearning for
God that he believed he had arrived in the other world."
This angelic music was for Saint Francis powerfully fortify-
ing, and his brother friars, to whom he recounted the
episode, bore witness. The version of Saint Bonaventure
and that of the *Legenda Perusina* agree in making this
angelic manifestation an event of listening in which nothing was given to be seen.[58] Only the version of the second
Consideration on the stigmata describes an apparition of
the angel with his viol and bow.[59]

This solitary act of listening to the invisible, which
already escapes the story—for how can one describe the
music of the angels?—would not seem to lend itself to any
image. Nevertheless this scene became a theme of
Franciscan iconography, certainly much less widespread
than that of the stigmatization of Saint Francis, but one
nevertheless that inspired numerous painters and
engravers.[60] The translation or transposition of the story
into an image can only be done by a radical chiasmus and
inversion: that which no one sees (the angel playing music)
is henceforth given to see for everyone—everyone, that is,
but Saint Francis himself, who is the addressee of this
angelic dispensation. We see more than does the saint of
the miracle, a miracle by which he alone is gratified. But he
alone hears this music, which is essentially and doubly hidden away because he alone heard it and because we are
talking about a painting. We who see without hearing see
him listening without seeing. It is a singular situation.

How, and where, can such paintings palpitate with
silence? Not in our vision of the angel musician, which

amounts to the common case of the pictorial representation of a musical scene, but in the face and the body of Saint Francis, who bears the profound silence of this hour. We see him listen to the silence, or that which for us is silence, even if it is visually explained, made explicit (sometimes, perhaps, too much so), which justifies certain corrections that some painters make to the letter of the story in order to be more faithful to its spirit. This act of listening often becomes a scene of ecstasy, which, in the end, as with Georges de La Tour, can do without the angel musician; or it can be situated outside, in a nocturnal and solitary landscape, even though all of the accounts specify that it took place inside, in the cell that sheltered the saint.[61] Such is the case in an Italian painting from the beginning of the seventeenth century by an unknown hand.[62] Saint Francis lies in a position of abandon and of profound lassitude, as if collapsed, legs spread apart, the left hand lowered toward the ground, without strength, and yet holding an upright crucifix that opposes its verticality to his declining weight. The nocturnal landscape is merely suggested in its unobtrusiveness and, in the upper left corner of the painting, in a luminous cloud, a *putto* plays the cithara. The light illuminating Francis comes from him. The right hand of the saint, raised in a gesture of openness and advancing into the foreground, forms a kind of second face. We catch the turning point, where the music resonates and makes Francis pass from exhaustion to thanksgiving. His face and his right side are turned toward the sky while the rest of his body has an uncommon gravity. To borrow the expression of Simone Weil, it is a matter of gravity and grace.

In the museum at the Chartreuse of Douai there is a work that was once attributed to Guercino and is presently attributed to a Florentine painter, Sigismondo Coccapani.[63] Here too, the scene takes place in nature. Saint Francis lies on the ground, with a skull at his feet, and a book has fallen from his hands. His exhausted face lies alongside a crucifix placed upon his shoulder, around which his arm passes weakly. Within this cluttered chiaroscuro there are two angels and two *putti*. One of the angels, above the saint, delicately and with compassion wipes his forehead with water. The other, the musician, plays his violin in a lively and joyful manner, reading from a part held and unrolled by a *putto* flying in front of him. His face is turned away from Saint Francis; he is totally absorbed by his music. As for Francis, his collapse is even more complete than in the painting at Rouen. His gaze absent and empty, he seems almost to be dying. The music that within the space of the painting resonates so close to his ears appears to come to him from far away, if it even comes to him, so much is he solitary and as if fallen into an abyss of silence. The load, or overload, of these figures almost stuck upon one another, allowing only a little bit of space and respiration, strongly underlines the absence of Saint Francis from the world, his interior silence become an act of listening to a music that is inaudible to us.

Francisco Ribalta, who, with his *Christ Embracing Saint Bernard in His Arms*, is the painter of one of the purest masterpieces of religious painting, was also inspired by angelic music.[64] He, for his part, held to the letter of the account. Saint Francis is on his bed in his cell, his hands raised and open, with an expression of profound, sudden emotion. A lamb, symbol of the Passion, stands upright with its feet upon the bed. Floating at the opposite extremity of the painting, swathed in a light and mobile drapery, an angel plays the lute. In the darkness at the back of the room, a friar enters at that very instant—the sole transgression of the narrative account, which Ribalta was not alone in allowing himself. As Jonathan Brown notes, the angel "points the lute like a crossbow at the recoiling body of the saint."[65] At the same time as the music, luminous rays come forth from the angel to envelop Saint Francis with their brightness. Francis looks up, but appears not to see the angel, though this is difficult to determine with certainty. Two diagonals go from the angel's face to the face of the saint, and from the angel's hands to the hands of the saint. It seems that Saint Francis is listening with his hands, as we might say of others that they speak with theirs. Less intensely mystical than the *Christ Embracing Saint Bernard,* this painting is nevertheless heavy with a pure silence, which it also gives to us to inhabit.

This silence is lost in the Venetian canvas of Carlo Saraceni.[66] The act of listening is replaced by a striking face-to-face encounter in which the music is nothing more than accessory. A beardless Saint Francis (which is very unusual), hands crossed upon his chest, fixes his eyes with devout attention upon the eyes of the feminine-featured angel who plays the violin just above him. At the feet of Francis an old friar, recumbent, is completely absorbed in the reading he is engaged in, and will have noticed nothing that is taking place around him. This is certainly the sign of the inaudible character of this music, and of the secret character of this encounter, but the eye is too distracted by the whole of the staging, by the still life in the foreground, with its two pairs of sandals, its drum, its basket, staff, etc. The encounter between the angel and Saint Francis has a specular aspect about it, which runs contrary to the act of listening: the angel forms a sort of double, young and feminine, to the face of Saint Francis.

Things are different in the great painting by Guercino, *Saint Francis and Saint Benedict with an Angel Musician,* which is in the Louvre.[67] The unwonted meeting of the two saints removes the scene from its context, and constitutes a powerful antithesis, but one that in fact weakens each of the two figures. His face raised toward the sky, and holding a tall crozier, Saint Benedict, majestic, appears to be all ears to the celestial concert. Saint Francis, at whom the neck of the angelic instrument is again pointed, turns his head away and raises his right hand, as if it were all too much, seemingly immersed in the imminence of the unbearable. This is indeed a scene of excess and of ecstasy. Francis is on the verge of fainting away, which recalls the account of the second Consideration on the stigmata, where it is written, "it seemed to him that, if the angel had drawn upon the bow a second time, his soul, by this intolerable sweetness, would be separated from his body."[68] In a more reduced format, Guercino offered two other versions of this work, in which the adventitious presence of Saint Benedict has been suppressed, and in which Saint Francis is alone with the angel.[69] The change offers the opportunity, by the empty space thus opened, for the appearance of a faraway nocturnal landscape, thus giving breathing space to the gaze and full resonance to the silent music. No one has shown the rending dimension of the gentlest music better than Guercino. As for Rilke, the beautiful is only the beginning of the terrible. Saint Francis is wounded more than healed by this music that we do not hear. The music stigmatizes him. And the visible exceeds itself, inviting us to pass beyond it. Indeed, there is a contradiction before our eyes between Francis's pained expression and the charm, full of consideration, of the angel musician. In no way can we see how this sweetness could wound. We must lend an ear and allow ourselves to be affected by the silence.

It sometimes happens that angelic music in painting is quite the contrary of silent; it becomes loud and ringing, intrusive, as in the work by Ambroise Frédeau entitled *Saint Nicolas of Tolentine Lulled by the Angels' Concert*.[70] Arms open wide, with one hand holding a crucifix, the saint, with an ecstatically joyful expression, finds himself in the midst of a veritable orchestra of angels. In front of him, behind him, above him there resounds the music of every sort of instrument: harp, organ, lute, transverse flute. . . . More strange than it is admirable, this work is one of profusion; it stands in contrast to the nocturnal Franciscan scene. One doesn't know where to look, nor to listen. There is a sense of intoxicated accumulation.

Let us leave it aside, without regret, a bit deafened, and with it the question of the unheard melodies of painting so that we can envisage another approach to silence.

One of the highest and most acute sites for the *contemplation of silence* in the Christian tradition is the contemplation of the Christ child. It has especially deepened as such in modern times, and particularly in the seventeenth century. In becoming incarnate and in assuming the human condition in its truth and plenitude, the divine Word from the outset also assumes that without which a man would not become, and would not be, a man: the state of childhood. The *Verbum infans* is Speech that does not speak, that cannot speak, Speech deprived of speech. In coming to reveal himself to us, the Word began by becoming silent. While our childhood is certainly a state of weakness, dependence, and precariousness, it also forms the preface and the prehistory to our speech to come: we are not deprived of that which we do not yet have. We do not have speech, but are already in it, we inhabit it already, we are, even before our birth, enveloped by it in every way. Things are otherwise for the incarnated Word. In effect he unites himself substantially with a human soul and body incapable of speaking, and which he could not make speak except through incongruous miracles that would be contrary to his mission. If the cult of the Child Jesus could sometimes, down through the ages, become a site of questionable and perhaps too human emotions and sentimentality, the seventeenth century saw in it above all a mystery of humiliation, just as meaningful and terrible as the cross.

Before returning to painting, it makes sense to listen to several spiritual authors of the French School who can teach us to see and to contemplate its silence. Cardinal de Bérulle devoted numerous mediations to the silence of the Word and of the Nativity, to "the eternal word of the Father who wills to be without speech."[71] For childhood constitutes "Jesus's most humble, most feeble, most helpless state."[72] Such a silence seems able only to call forth our own: "It is not for us to speak of this mystery; we are to admire and to adore it through a profound silence, rather than to profane and to debase it with our weak thoughts.

Jesus is a child and, in obligation to silence, he cannot speak to us about it; instead, it is up to the Virgin and to the angel serving Jesus to speak of it to us."[73] But is it certain that one must fall silent when Jesus himself is vowed to silence? "So long as the Son of God is in silence and even helpless to speak because of his childhood, we must speak for him and we must speak of him, all the more willingly in that it is for us that he is in this humble state of silence and helplessness; for by his own being and by his eternal birth he is the power, the word, and the wisdom of his Father."[74] At the conclusion of these lines Bérulle composes one of the most powerful hymns to silence ever written, a hymn to the silence of Mary, to her "life of silence which adores the eternal word." Mary, "seeing before her eyes, on her breast, in her arms, this very word, the substantial word of the Father, mute and reduced to silence by the state of his childhood," silently raises herself out of silence.[75]

In the same Oratorian tradition, François Bourgoing opposes the brief helplessness of the cross and the long helplessness of Christ's childhood: "On the cross, Jesus was deprived of the effects of his power and his glory, but not of his wisdom nor of speech, for he spoke there; but in the manger he said not a word, he spoke not. The Shepherds hailed him, the Magi came from the East to adore him, and yet this divine wisdom manifested itself not at all, the Word of God became silent."[76] And Bourgoing invokes soon after the very body of the child Jesus, in a sort of *blason* of weakness:

> O mouth of Jesus, that is the fountain of Paradise from which *the rivers of living water* spring, which is to say, the *words that are spirit and life,* and that nevertheless is mute in the manger! O hands of Jesus, that by their touch heal the sick, and are nevertheless enveloped in swaddling clothes! O attractive eyes of Jesus, that by their gaze convert souls, and yet in this early childhood are either open wide with tears, or closed by sleep![77]

Even into the eighteenth century, the Jesuit father Jean
Nicholas Grou, who also translated Plato into French, was
making the same sorts of invocations:

> Reason loses itself here, it must adore, and hold itself in
> silence. A God suffers, a God cries; the Almighty endures
> all the weaknesses of childhood, he cannot help himself by
> any movement, he can only express himself by inarticulate
> cries. He is eternal wisdom, but he does not even have the
> use of speech, and he gives no sign at all by which one
> might distinguish him from ordinary children.[78]

If the *Nativity,* the *Adoration of the Shepherds,* and the
Adoration of the Magi are among the most established
themes in painting, these works are often very far from
encouraging us to contemplate silence and meditate upon
the *Verbum infans.* There are glorious and musical examples, but there are also humble and silent ones, close to the
spirit of the words cited above. Thus Domenichino, in an
Adoration of the Shepherds full of astonishment and jubila-
tion, places in the foreground, in profile, a bagpipe player
with cheeks almost as swollen as the bladders of his instrument, which was a decidedly strange idea.[79] Similarly
Zurbaran, while emphasizing the prayerful concentration
of Joseph as well as that of other characters, shows Jesus
with open eyes gazing toward us with a look that draws
attention and manifests him for what he is. In the sky, looking toward him, a majestic angel, clothed all in red, plays
the harp. And on the earth itself next to Mary, there are also
angel musicians. One plays the lute and the other sings
with the help of a score. Songs of earth and songs of heaven
accompany the vigilant silence of Jesus.[80]

Completely different, and scrupulously in conformity
with the spirit of the French School, is the *Adoration of the
Shepherds* by Georges de La Tour, at the Louvre. In a space
so confined (and which is even more so due to the fact that
the canvas has been mutilated), there is yet an ample breath
of silence. Jesus is the light of the world, but here, far from
being a source of brightness as in numerous other nativities,

he is the light that needs to be illuminated. Only the candle that Joseph both holds out and obscures shows him to us, and illuminates the entire scene. This familiar gesture in de La Tour, which can turn into a trick, here takes on a deeper meaning: it gathers in the significance of the scene in its entirety. The manifestation of the child Jesus is itself an oblique manifestation, and an obscured light. Instead of being naked or barely clothed as is often the case in painting, the child Jesus—in conformity with practices of the artist's time, it is true—is swaddled in such a way that he seems like a little mummy. Only his face is uncovered—all his members are closely imprisoned by the cloth wrapped around him, he is radically powerless to make any movement. He is exactly consistent with the description that Bourgoing will give. And he who forms the center of all the gazes around him has his eyes closed: Jesus is sound asleep, he in his humanity is not present to those who are present to him, which adds helplessness to helplessness, and secret to secret. Even the lamb, with its bright gaze, has more presence than he. Jesus is almost anonymous, nothing signals that he is unusual, except perhaps for the devotion of those who surround him. He is truly the *hidden God*.

Of the five adults, only Mary is expressly prayerful, with her hands joined, but all are intensely silent. If it is true that, as Jacques Thuillier says,[81] the smile of the shepherd at the center, with a flute in his hand, is the only smile without ambiguity in the entire œuvre of Georges de La Tour, it above all points up the extreme gravity, attentive and collected, of the other characters. They adore the silent Word in silence, in silence and by silence. But this silence, in every respect, is central: even if it is a human candle, and not a supernatural light that illuminates the body of Jesus, it is only by the grace of Jesus, by the power of this mute and sleeping child, that these adults are thus assembled to pray and to adore. They depend on him who depends on them. They who hover over him and seem to look after him nevertheless exist only because of him. It is they who belong to him. And their silence too belongs to him, to his own silence as source and origin; he is not their work nor their accomplishment, he is already a gift received from the one who seems to do nothing and to be unable to do anything. He is the Master of silence, and they are only his servants. This canvas gives a lesson in silence, one that is all the stronger in that it has avoided the marvelous and the romantic, and has required that everything in it be *common*, and thus capable of being shared and retold by us.

This silent contemplation of the silent Word could bear the title that Olivier Messiaen gave to one of his *Vingt regards sur l'Enfant Jésus*, the seventeenth: *Regard du silence (Gaze of Silence)*. It can lead to other dimensions of silence in painting, the various forms of attention and of listening in which the act of making silence gives itself to be seen in the face and body. We have already encountered one in the attention of Saint Francis of Assisi to the music heard only by him, but there are others that are more common. Thus the many readers, male and female, in the history of painting! From biblical characters to small anonymous schoolboys, situated in the desert or in the intimacy of a comfortable room, how many paintings have shown this scrutiny of the written, which seems to cause us to absent ourselves from that which surrounds us! These are paintings of absorption, according to Michael Fried's term, who studies absorption in eighteenth-century painting, though by his own admission the tradition dates much earlier.[82] In the curious pages in which he describes readers glimpsed in trains or libraries, Patrick Drevet shows nicely how this absorption can in turn absorb us: "The act of reading renders the body of the person engaged in it an object of enigma. In the midst of others, it gives that body a visibility that sets it up as an icon. It gives it a degree of appearance that is excessive, and insistent."[83] Drevet sees in the orientation of the entire body "toward the unique tension of the gaze, a kind of figure of relinquishment, and even of nudity."[84] The silence of the attention to the invisible by means of the eyes forms a silence that intensely gives itself to be seen, and its nudity has fascinated painters.

But there is another silence of attention, that of listening to human speech. In a fine study on "Rembrandt and the Spoken Word," Julius Held notes, following Bauch, that the actions proper to the works of Rembrandt are human speech and human listening.[85] And above all he shows that Rembrandt deviates from traditional representations of the exchange of words, where gesturing often gives the impression that two people are speaking at the same time. "In most situations," writes Held, "where Rembrandt chose to render a dialogue between two people he permits only one to talk; the other is there to listen. This mute presence serves, thanks to the precise fixing in time and the differentiation of individual attitudes, to sharpen the psychological effect of the action."[86] A good example, judiciously analyzed by Held, is the engraving of Christ preaching, known by the name of *La Petite Tombe*.[87] The subject is not a specific episode from the Gospels, but one day among many of Jesus' preaching.

As always, Rembrandt unveils here the daily character of the extraordinary, and the extraordinary character of the quotidian. The audience, fairly numerous but close, is gathered in a circle around Christ. With the exception of the young man seated at his feet and, in the foreground, a child lying on his belly and tracing, with his left hand, signs in the dust (the only one who hears without listening), this audience is rather old. Whether they be heavy or on the contrary emaciated, the marked faces of the auditors of Jesus have nothing ideal about them, nor is there that conventional beauty that painters often spread over religious scenes. Some are seated or crouching, others are standing; some are looking toward Jesus and others staring into the void; but they all bear on their faces and in their postures the marks of an extreme attention, and thus of a profound silence as well. What makes this silence beautiful is that it has nothing of a sudden silence about it—the silence of an instant of shock or of stupefaction, like those that would be elicited by a word or a phrase that would all of the sudden bowl us over. This engraving in effect bears duration within it.

There are two gestures that appear rather linked to the instant: one, on the left, of a mature man wearing a sort of beret, who scratches his lip with his thumb, as if perplexedly questioning himself; and one on the right, an old man with a long beard, who stares at Jesus while bending his torso forward, as if caught up by his words. Aside from these, the postures of the other characters are of the sort that one does not adopt at the beginning of a speech, but rather that one winds up taking, each person having his own, when one has been listening for a long time and is prepared to listen for even longer. Curled up, sunken, or firmly planted on the ground, the bodies in their efforts at attention are folded in upon themselves and immobile. Only Jesus' body offers itself and opens itself while speaking, the feet spread apart and perpendicular, the arms raised, showing the palms, with a movement that contrasts with the inclination of his somewhat heavy head. He too listens, and he speaks only because he listens, for the words that he says he does not say on his own.[88] They are not from him, but from the Father who sent him.[89] A historian said of this admirable engraving: "Rembrandt here accomplished the impossible: he made the portrait of a voice."[90] But the portrait of a voice can be made only by showing us the dimension of silence from which it proceeds and the dimension of silence to which it addresses itself: this is what Rembrandt understood so profoundly.

The act of listening is aimed not only at the spoken word, but can also be aimed at nature, in particular when nature is thought of as having its own life and as forming a visible word addressed to us by God. This listening, too, is devoted to silence. Such is the case in the paintings of Caspar David Friedrich. It is God he seeks to hear in the silence of nature; Carl Gustav Carus says the same in his *Nine Letters on Landscape Painting*.[91] Carus was not satisfied by the expression "landscape painting" and would have liked to replace it by *Erdlebenbildkunst*, the art of showing the life of the earth.[92] For him, nature is already in herself so alive and so full of meaning that "animated creatures . . . are in this sense foreign to and useless in a landscape," except in those cases where they "contribute, by making evident the meaning of other elements, to reinforce to a great degree the effect that these produce."[93] This principle holds for him not only for animals, but for human figures as well: these can only be nature's foil.

How would the image of man not be superfluous when the landscape itself is already completely re-formed by the human mind? This exclusion of man is not equivalent to the exclusion of anthropocentrism—quite the contrary. It remains that a principle of strict subordination is laid down in the relation of man to the landscape. Among the examples that Carus takes to illustrate his remarks, one is particularly important for Friedrich's painting: "A solitary figure, lost in the contemplation of a peaceful expanse, will incite the man who looks upon the painting to identify himself with that figure." These figures, seen from afar and, most frequently, from behind are our ambassadors and our representatives within the space of the landscape. We are not so much invited to *see them* (and, after all, there is very little of them to see) as to *see through them*, or *as they see*. The work of Friedrich at once both accomplishes and gives the lie to that fine legend of the Chinese artist who, after having painted a landscape, entered into it, withdrew, and disappeared: he is, most often, already *in* the painting, and we with him, but his purpose is to remain there, listening to silence, and not to disappear.

Regarding these figures, Marcel Brion, in the fine pages he devoted to Friedrich, said: "One guesses that, as minuscule as they are, they possess a considerable importance, a meaning that we should not allow to escape; otherwise, the space of the landscape would dissipate at the same time."[94] Without them, the silence would no longer be able to be heard, there would not even be any more silence. Brion adds that, for Friedrich, the human figure "has for its object to give, materially, the scale of the landscape, and, even more, to suggest to the spectator its *spiritual scale.*"[95] The famous *Monk at the Seashore,* which so captivated Kleist and many others, demonstrates this point clearly. This tiny figure, on a narrow strip of sand, on the shore of a somber sea, supports all by himself the stormy horizon and the weight of the immense sky. The painting is only silent by virtue of his presence. Pascal's phrase, with its powerful rhythm, seems fitting here: "The eternal silence of these infinite spaces fills me with dread."[96] In the deictic "these" a human body makes itself present, in front of these spaces, showing them, perceiving them, listening to and bearing their silence. At issue is not a simple spiritual consideration. It is the "these" that gives the scale of the silence. A page of declamation could not make us hear it and what is frightening about it so well as this demonstrative monosyllable.

This appears clearly if we compare Friedrich's painting with a study of Constable that, in many respects, is quite similar.[97] In this small, very horizontal study, we find a narrow beach, a green sea, and a windy and turbulent sky. But on the sea there are boats, one near, the other moving away—Friedrich had initially put boats in the *Monk on the Seashore,* and then covered over them—and on the beach, in the foreground, two women walking. Taking up Brion's distinction, they give the material scale of the landscape, but not its spiritual scale. Constable's study is thoroughly beautiful, but it is about a walk on the beach on a gray day, and not about the contemplation of the silence of nature. These two women walking take the air; they do not scrutinize the divine expression in things.

The *Woman at Sunset* or the *Traveler Contemplating a Sea of Clouds* are in contemplation: the first, with a gesture of prayer, concealing from us the sun that outlines her silhouette; the second, on a promontory.[98] This listening to silence does not lose its rootedness in human history. As Anne Hollander has remarked, however allegorical Friedrich's paintings may be, he does not fall into the facile habit of representing his characters either with a mythological nudity or in ideal and intemporal clothing: the costume of his characters is precisely dated and datable, it is that of Friedrich's time, and it itself escapes from all allegorizing.[99] There is more strength there than in symbols torn from history. A work by Ferdinand Hodler, *Gaze into the Beyond*,[100] inverts Friedrich's *Traveler*, and in so doing loses the silence in which the latter stands. At the summit of a rocky peak, surmounting the sea of clouds out of which are glimpsed in the distance parallel lines of crests that barely emerge, there stands a naked young man, his body in a perfect symmetry, seen from the front, his hands flat over his breast. It is he, above all else, that Hodler gives to be seen; and this regular body, foreign to any history, is nothing more than a naked soul, as in the myths of Plato. There is no longer any silence to listen to. Whatever reservations one might be inclined to have toward Friedrich's paintings, it must be admitted that he always kept himself from falling into this danger.

Of all these silences, and of the many others with which visible works pulse, is it necessary to single out a silence in painting itself, which would belong only to modernity, and which would be of a piece with painting's approach to its proper essence, with the birth of "pure" painting, actively excluding everything foreign to it, including all of that with which history and various institutions have continually mingled it? This is Georges Bataille's thesis in the book that he wrote on Manet, which is not without its dignity.[101] Manet's work and project mark, in the strict sense of the term, an epoch establishing silence in painting. Bataille concedes that, regarding this silence, one cannot "not see a gleam appear" in certain previous works, nor indeed "perhaps a little bit everywhere in painting,"[102] but it remains that there is "a new form of painting . . . that no one foresaw, and that only the strange reactions and the risky, anguished searching of Edouard Manet attained."[103] Even Goya, whom this dramaturgical vision of history proposes for a moment as another candidate for the paternity of pictorial silence, is finally thrust aside from this title, by often specious arguments.

The lively and mocking spirit of Georges Duthuit, who was sometimes led off course by his taste for polemics, vigorously criticized these theses, in large part inspired by Malraux, according to which Manet had inaugurated "painting having nothing else to love, to understand, or to signify than its proper signs."[104] He denounces the apophatism and the acosmism of such approaches, just as in his *Le musée inimaginable* he criticizes "the reign of the man who is sovereign over the world, sovereign to the point where he has made it disappear."[105] But the decisive question, beyond that of knowing if or to what point Manet, in a sort of prophetic solitude, is the founder of twentieth-century painting, bears here in particular upon the meaning of this silence and upon its radical newness. What does Georges Bataille say about this silence?

It is a matter of "the transformation of painting, of the language or discourse it was, into the autonomous art . . . it has been since Manet's time . . . ; bizarre as it is, the concern was the silence of painting." But, in this first formulation, the autonomy of painting is its *musical* development: it must be "autonomous—liberated in the same degree as music from the functions of discourse," in order that the painter might "give himself freely to the art of painting, to technique, to the song of forms and colors."[106] Poetry or music? The debate is an ancient one. And complex, too, because to describe the silence of one of Manet's paintings, Bataille cites Verlaine's *Art poétique:* "Take hold of eloquence and wring its neck."[107] That "silence reigns" signifies that "art is the supreme value" and that "the work of art here takes the place of everything that in the past . . . was sacred and majestic."[108]

The relation of this "silence" to narration is in truth complex, and becomes dialectical. Sometimes Manet characterizes himself for Bataille by his renunciation of all narration, and sometimes by the act of narrating in a different way. But a different narration is not the other of all narration. "It is true," writes Bataille, "that Manet's painting recounts, it recounts no less than that of Goya. But with indifference toward what it is recounting."[109] These words are written with regard to the *Execution of Maximilien,* and are largely contestable, and were indeed contested. Indifference to the "subject" signifies that the subject is nothing more than a *"pretext* for the painting," and Bataille concludes: "All pretext of eloquence, feigned or genuine, is eliminated. There remain spots of different colors and the misleading impression that a feeling ought to be born from the subject: it is the strange impression of an absence." But the indifference toward that which one recounts is still a relation with what one recounts, and a precise mode of narration, not a rupture with narration. As for "the impression of absence," it puts intensely into play that which absents itself (this is the very definition of all privation, in the Aristotelian sense), and thus gives to the "subject," if the analysis is true, a considerable importance.

These criteria would not for all of that characterize either the beauty or the modernity of a pictorial work: we have all seen dozens of paintings depicting biblical scenes in which it is quite apparent, whether or not the piece was a commission, that the "subject" had only been a "pretext," and in which the painter's indifference is noticeable. "The strange impression of an absence" assuredly emerges: that of the absence of any spirituality. Are such paintings therefore foundational of modernity? These are purely negative criteria, by themselves insufficient. Besides, does this silence, defined as rupture with discourse, give itself to be heard as silence? What we encounter in this "silence" is in fact *discourse,* the discourse of the religion of art or of art as a new religion, art as a "supreme value." It is thus a talkative silence, a silence that gives lessons, that disabuses, or claims to disabuse, of everything except itself. Bataille in vain affirms that "from now on, what is sacred is mute";[110] throughout his book he gives speech to this muteness, and this speech is a metaphysical thesis: art becomes sacred, and the only thing that is sacred, when it ceases to be in the world in order to enter into the no man's land of the museum. The museum as site of insignificance, at the same time that it becomes the site of a cult, delivers the thesis of any objection ever imaginable.

To whomever would object that painting has never reduced itself to discourse nor to eloquence, and that Manet, whatever his genius, could not inaugurate a silence that preceded him, the response is that ever since Manet we can no longer see or know what painting was before him, for because of him, painting has become, for us, alike to his. "The beauty of older painting is for us, now, alike to that of modern painting." It has entered "into a silence alike to his."[111] But then how would one know that painting did not already have this silence, and how would one know that Manet accomplished a rupture in the history of art? There is too much granting here of what needs to be demonstrated—that is, that painting before Manet was discursive, and that it no longer is.

More fundamentally, a clear alternative appears: either painting is in its essence discursive, and thus language (and in this case we do not see how it could ever cease to be so), or its capacity to become rhetorical and talkative forms a deviation with relation to its immanent project, and, in this case, silence has always inhabited it, and is the very norm against which the departures, however frequent they may be at such and such moment in history, can be measured. In what way is the painting of Chardin more discursive than that of Manet? In a parallel order, one can consider that the rupture of poetry with narration, didacticism, and eloquence in the second half of the nineteenth century is a major event; but one only need read the Chinese poets of the golden age to see that this possibility has always belonged to poetry. As Henri Maldiney has shown so forcefully, "It is a mistake to say that art is a language, for . . . in art signification and manifestation are one. . . . In art, forms speak, not signs. The form signifies *itself*, and signifies by appearing."[112]

Ever since there has been painting, man has translated his listening to the silence of the world into forms. For every act of listening responds, and it is with his hands that the painter responds, in turn giving something to listen to. Painting makes us inhabit silence: that of the world, a musical silence. Cézanne, according to Gasquet, said of Veronese: "Things, beings entered into his soul with the sunshine, without anything that separates them from the light, without design, without abstractions, all in colors. They came out one day, the same, but, we don't know why, clothed in a soft glory. Happy, as if they had breathed a mysterious music,"[113] which we hear "radiate" from the canvases. If we can listen to pictorial works, it is because the painter is himself or herself as much made up of listening as of vision—otherwise he or she would not be a human being. To finish, let us leave the word to Cézanne, who said of the painter: "All his will must be of silence. He must make silent within himself all the voices of preconceptions, forget, forget, make silence, be a perfect echo."[114]

NOTES

1. Lessing, *Laocoön*, 4–5.
2. Aristotle, *De Anima*, II, 10, 422 A 23–24.
3. Claudel, *L'Œil écoute*, in *Œuvres en prose*, 167. Cf. 173: "I believe that we would better understand the Dutch landscapes, these themes of contemplation, these sources of silence, which owe their origin less to curiosity than to reflection, if we learned to open our ears to them at the same time that, with our eyes, we feed our intelligence upon them." tran. Bell, *The Eye Listens*, 8 [translation modified].

4. Claudel, *Le soulier de satin*, IV, 2, in *Théâ:* . t. II, 871.

5. Bataille, *Manet*, 60; tran. Wainhouse and Emmons, 64 [translation modified].

6. Bataille, *Manet*, 88; tran. Wainhouse and Emmons, 102 [translation modified].

7. Bataille, *Manet*, 73–76; tran. Wainhouse and Emmons, p. 86 [translation modified].

8. John Keats, *Ode on a Grecian Urn*, lines 1–2.

9. Cf. Wasserman, *The Finer Tone*, 16–17, which on the contrary attenuate, strangely, the reach of these terms.

10. *Ode*, lines 3–4

11. Cf. Vendler, *The Odes of John Keats*, 118.

12. *Ode*, line 10.

13. *Ode*, lines 11–14.

14. Wasserman, *Finer Tone*, 44.

15. *Ode*, lines 23–24.

16. Mallarmé, *Œuvres complètes*, t. I, 199; tran. Weinfeld, *Collected Poems*, 43 [translation slightly modified]. Cf. Richard, *L'univers imaginaire de Mallarmé*, 65: "All the antique decor introduced into the final miracle of a living silence and a singing emptiness, of a music that has died away, yet is still sensible: the music which emanates from the poem itself."

17. Cf. Vendler, *Odes*, 312 n. 18.

18. *Ode*, lines 49–50.

19. Vendler, *Odes*, 147.

20. Pater, *The Renaissance*, 157. For Pater, all art tends to the condition of music: music is the aim of all art.

21. Ibid., 158.

22. Russell, *Claude Lorrain*, 91–93. This picture, sometimes attributed to Paul Bril, is in Providence.

23. This painting can be found in Washington, D.C. Cf. Westermann, *Le siècle d'or en Hollande*, 158–61.

24. Quoted in Russell, *Claude Lorrain*, 92.

25. Tomatis, *Ecouter l'univers*, 127.

26. Musée de Nancy; see Russell, *Claude Lorrain*, 124–25.

27. New York. Cf. Homer, *Thomas Eakins*, 145.

28. 1923, Paris, Musée Picasso.

29. Cf., for example, Clement of Alexandria, *Protrepticus*, I, 5, 3.

30. Plutarch, *De Iside et Osiride*, 2; tran. Babbitt, *Isis and Osiris* in *Moralia*, V, §68, 159.

31. Plutarch, *Œuvres morales*, V, *Isis et Osiris*; ed. and trans. Froidefond, 272, 313.

32. Levey, *Painting and Sculpture*, 132–34. The sculpture is at the Louvre.

33. Quoted by Leroy-Jay-Lemaistre, *Musée du Louvre*, 123.

34. Diderot, *Salon de 1765*, 120.

35. Mallarmé, *Œuvres complètes*, t. I, 326; tran. Weinfield, 80.

36. Plotinus, *Enneads*, I:4, 16; tran. Armstrong, *Plotinus*, 1: 211 [translation modified].

37. Arasse, *Le détail*, 170.

38. Cf. Hibbard, *Caravaggio*, 155.

39. Ibid., 36.

40. Cf. Schneider, *Les natures mortes*, 172.

41. Sterling, *La nature morte*, 59.

42. Rodenbach, *Choix de poésies*, 122.

43. Aristotle, *Physics*, II, 1, 192 B 16.

44. The painting is in the Louvre. Cf. Rosenberg, *Chardin 1699–1779*, 340.

45. Diderot, *Salon de 1765*, 117.

46. Ibid., 120.

47. Ponge, *Nouveau recueil*, 167–175.

48. Ibid., 171.

49. Ibid., 168.

50. Michel and Rosenberg, *Subleyras*, 166–67.

51. Sterling, *La nature morte*, 85.

52. Apollinaire, *Chroniques d'art*, 77.

53. Quoted by Sterling, *La nature morte*, 102. Cf. Sabatier, *Mirors de la musique*, 443.

54. Cf. Daix and Vallier, *Georges Braque*, 27:78–79.

55. Ibid., 86:182–83.

56. Ibid., 98.

57. Thomas of Celano, *Vita secunda*, 89, 129, in Desbonnets and Vorreux, ed., *Saint François d'Assise*, 452.

58. Bonaventure, *Legenda major*, 5, 11, in Desbonnets and Vorreux, ed., *Saint François d'Assise*, 629; *Legenda Perusina*, 24, in Desbonnets and Vorreux, ed., *Saint François d'Assise*, 898–99.

59. Desbonnets and Vorreux, ed., *Saint François d'Assise*, 1346.

60. Cf. Gieben, "Saint François dans l'art populaire et l'art graphique," in *Saint François et ses frères*, 433–37.

61. Cf. Gieben, *Saint François et ses frères*, 433, on Francesco Vanni.

62. Musée de Rouen. Cf. Lavergnée, *Seicento*, 385–86.

63. Forneris, *La musique et la peinture*, 28–29.

64. Prado, Madrid. Cf. Brown, *Golden Age of Painting*, 110–12.

65. Ibid., 112.

66. Church of the Redeemer, Venice.

67. Cf. Mahon, *Il Guercino*, 134–35.

68. Desbonnets and Vorreux, ed., *Saint François d'Assise*, 1346.

69. One is found at Dresden and the other at Warsaw. Cf. Mahon, *Il Guercino*, 136, 172.

70. At Toulouse. Cf. Forneris, *La musique et la peinture*, 32–33.

71. Bérulle, *Opuscules de piété*, no. 57, §5, 218.

72. Ibid., no. 58, §1, 226.

73. Ibid., no. 59, §5, 231.

74. Ibid., no. 60, §1, 233.

75. Ibid., no. 60, §3, 233.

76. Bourgoing, *Méditations sur les vérités*, t. 1, 446–47.

77. Ibid., 449.

78. Grou, *L'intérieur de Jésus et de Marie*, t. II, 228–29.

79. Edinburgh.

80. Grenoble. Cf. J. Brown, *Golden Age of Painting*, 168–70.

81. Thuillier, *Georges de La Tour*, 200.

82. Fried, *Absorption and Theatricality*, chap. 1. Cf. 43.

83. Drevet, *Petites études sur le désir de voir*, II:14.

84. Ibid., 38.

85. Held, "Rembrandt and the Spoken Word," 164–83.

86. Ibid., 172.

87. Cf. Bussière, *Rembrandt, Eaux-fortes*, 224–25; and Held, "Rembrandt and the Spoken Word," 177–78.

88. John 14:10.

89. John 14:24.

90. A Hyatt Major, cited by Bussière, *Rembrandt, Eaux-fortes*, 224.

91. Cf. the French translation of these letters by Dickenherr et al. in Carus and Friedrich, *De la peinture*, 76–77: "Beauty is nothing other than that which provokes the sensation of the divine essence in nature, which is to say in the world of sensible phenomena." Cf. the analysis of Rosenblum, *Modern Painting and the Northern Romantic Tradition*, chap. 1.

92. Carus and Friedrich, *De la peinture*, 108–9.

93. Ibid., 75–76 (and for the quotation that follows).

94. Brion, *Peinture romantique*, 146.

95. Ibid., 160–61. Cf. Rosenblum, *Modern Painting*, 21–22.

96. Pascal, *Pensées*, Brunschvicg §206; Lafuma §201; tran. Krailsheimer, 66.

97. John Constable, *The Beach at Brighton, 12 June 1824*, Victoria and Albert Museum, London. Cf. Meyer, *Les maîtres du paysage anglais*, 155.

98. At Essen and at Hamburg, respectively. Sunset, or sunrise? Various authors indicate the one or the other.

99. Hollander, *Seeing Through Clothes*, 426.

100. Cf. Rosenblum, *Modern Painting*, 125.

101. Bataille, *Manet*; tran. Wainhouse and Emmons. James H. Rubin's book, *Manet's Silence and the Poetics of Bouquets*, takes up the idea, as his title shows, but, strangely, never mentions Bataille's book.

102. Bataille, *Manet*, 45; tran. Wainhouse and Emmons, 50.

103. Bataille, *Manet*, 43–44; tran. Wainhouse and Emmons, 49 [translation modified].

104. Duthuit, *L'image et l'instant*, 78. Chapter V evokes Manet's art positively, and chapter VI, "Manet a-t-il existé?" ("Did Manet Exist?") critiques Bataille's theses.

105. Duthuit, *Le musée inimaginable*, t. II, 311.

106. Bataille, *Manet*, 35; tran. Wainhouse and Emmons, 36–37 [translation modified].

107. Bataille, *Manet*, 48; tran. Wainhouse and Emmons, 52 [translation modified].

108. Bataille, *Manet*, 60, cf. 69; tran. Wainhouse and Emmons, 64, cf. 71 [translation modified].

109. Bataille, *Manet*, 48, as for the quotations that follow; tran. Wainhouse and Emmons, 51, 52 [translations modified].

110. Bataille, *Manet*, 52; tran. Wainhouse and Emmons, 58.

111. Bataille, *Manet*, 53; tran. Wainhouse and Emmons, 58 [translation modified].

112. Maldiney, *Regard, Parole, Espace*, 250; cf. 131.

113. Doran, *Conversations avec Cézanne*, 132.

114. Ibid., 109.

A Polyptych of Slumbers

THE BODY of the sleeping human being is no longer responsible for its own visibility. It is certainly present to the world, for instance as long as it breathes, but it no longer seems to give proof of its presence. It appears, but without standing up to account for its appearance, without attesting by its gaze that it comes of its own accord before our gaze. The manifestation of the body is transformed through and through, in a manner that is not merely privative, as if this body lacked vigilant presence, for this deficiency also makes the body inhabit the world differently, and deliver itself to a gaze differently. As annoyed as we might be when someone catches us asleep, it is a possibility to which we have consented, in law and in general, by closing our eyes, and by abandoning ourselves to sleep. To fall asleep is also to accept no longer watching over our manifestation, and no longer supervising ourselves.

This surrender has its charms. Poetry and literature have often evoked them. Thus we have Proust in *La prisonnière* speaking of Albertine's sleep: "I have spent charming evenings talking, playing games with Albertine, but never any so pleasant as when I was watching her sleep. Granted that she might have, as she chatted with me, or played cards, that spontaneity which no actress could have imitated, it was a spontaneity carried to the second degree that was offered me by her sleep."[1] Sleep would constitute the revelation of this natural paradox hidden beneath the natural spontaneity: we believe, doubtless a bit too quickly, that this body has returned to the state of nature. To such a point, indeed, that the sleeping body can wind up being considered as if it were a landscape: "It was a whole psychological existence that was spread out before me, for me; as I used to remain for hours lying on the beach, in the moonlight, so long could I have remained there gazing at her, listening to her."[2]

Still, whatever the reveries, especially erotic ones, to which such contemplation lends itself, it seems that, unlike dreams, which are a phenomenon of great complexity and indefinite richness of meaning, sleep is poor and monotonous. While it may pose decisive questions for neurophysiology, it nonetheless in many respects neutralizes the singularity of human beings. Nothing resembles a sleeper so much as another sleeper, and the postures of sleep do not have the subtle meanings that history and social life confer upon our waking gestures. Doesn't sleep have for its sole end the giving of rest from our fatigue and the restoration of our strength? Are there many ways to show a sleeping body? Certainly, it can be handsome or ugly, healthy or sick, young or old, clothed or naked, but, insofar as it is asleep, it presents, it would seem, a certain invariance. The variations that painting might make upon the theme of sleep would thus be merely stylistic variations, which would not place different sorts of slumber into play, nor various, or even opposed, meanings of sleep; they would form only diverse ways to show the same human being. But this is all just preconceptions.

Sleep's interruption of our active commerce with the world always takes place in a significant situation, and always forms the scansion of a history. What is suspended at that moment belongs to this suspense itself, and confers upon it a range that differs each time. Popular language, which speaks of the "sleep of the righteous," supposing too easily that it would not be troubled or that it would be the sleep of a "peaceful conscience," demonstrates this well. Greek mythology, on one hand, and biblical history, on the other, have given painting the opportunity and the task of evoking various slumbers fraught with often contrary meanings.

There is to begin with sleep as the site for a revelation or for a communication with the divine via a dream: the sleep of Jacob at Bethel, for instance, where God binds himself to Jacob by his promises;[3] or the sleep of King Solomon at Gibeon, where he receives the gift of discernment, which he will put into action immediately after in his famous judgment;[4] or the sleep of Joseph, the spouse of Mary, wherein Jesus' immaculate conception and messianic character are revealed to him.[5] Contrasting with these, the Scriptures also describe the shameful and scorn-worthy sleep of a drunken and naked Noah, surprised by his sons.[6] In the New Testament, two slumbers form a chiasmus: that of Jesus in the boat, sleeping while the apostles watch and become frantic at the storm that rises and threatens them,[7] and that of the apostles at Gethsemane, when Jesus had asked them to stay awake with him.[8] There are still others. All these scenes put into play incomparable possibilities of sleep and of the sleeping being.

Mythology also has its slumbers, which have inspired many painters: the erotic slumbers of Mars or of Venus; the eternal sleep of Endymion in the clear moonlight; the sleep of Ariane at Naxos, which Theseus takes advantage of in order to abandon her before Dionysos executes his designs upon her . . . No enumeration could be exhaustive, seeing as sleep in painting obviously is not limited to mythological or religious scenes. Certain painters, such as Courbet, experience a predilection for, if not a fascination with, the representation of the sleeping body. And, doubtless, this can be said of certain historical periods, too, even if no single period is uninterested in the topic.[9] What can painting show about the sleeping body? What can it teach us of the diversity of slumbers? How does it make a presence, or an act of presence, out of absence? Several works only will have to serve as points of reference and sites for our gaze.

Giving oneself up to sleep can constitute the worst of abandonments, wherein we abandon another person to his solitude and his distress by withdrawing ourselves from the common world and from our community with him. Our eyelids close upon our weary gaze, and our ears become deaf to the other's voice. One can thus leave someone without even moving away simply by dozing off. The being who is asleep, however physically close he may be, stays in the inaccessible distance of his withdrawal. In the most sorrowful hour, during which he pronounced the definitive and complete "Yes" to his Passion for the salvation of men, Jesus was, despite himself, alone. He who often sought solitude to pray and thus to withdraw from his disciples asks at Gethsemane, when all the possible forms of darkness are thickening and growing heavy, that they stay awake with him and pray. Judas has already betrayed him, but Peter, James, and John betray him by falling asleep.

The synoptic gospels present several variants in the account of this scene. In Matthew and Mark, Jesus finds his disciples asleep and awakens them three times running, while in Luke this takes place only once. Luke is also the only one to mention the apparition to Jesus of a consoling angel, as well as the bloody sweat. In Luke, Jesus is on his knees, while in the two other synoptic gospels he falls to the ground.

Numerous paintings have depicted this decisive scene. The iconography presents two major possibilities, according to the importance conferred upon the peccaminous sleep of the apostles. Sometimes we do not see the apostles at all, or barely, and all the attention is concentrated on the prayerful solitude of Christ. Delacroix made this choice, both in his large youthful painting, which is in the Church of Saint-Paul in Paris, as well as in a later and stronger work in which Christ is collapsed upon the ground. The disciples do not appear, or we only perceive their presence secondarily or fragmentarily.[10] Certain painters oscillate between two possibilities: El Greco, who gave several versions of *Christ in the Olive Garden,* always represents the three apostles plunged in sleep. But, in one case, they occupy the entire foreground, along with incredible draperies seemingly lifted by the wind, which increase the weight of their presence and of their sleep;[11] while, in another, Christ is in the foreground, face to face with the angel bearing the chalice, separating the crowd led by Judas who comes from faraway toward him on the right, from, on the left, the apostles asleep, in the middle ground, just below the angel.[12] Certainly, each time, the deficiency of human presence to Jesus is underscored, as well as the fact that he is caught between two betrayals; but what is capital in the first version is only secondary in the other.

How is this sleep, which denies Jesus just as surely as a spoken denial, given to be seen? Three Venetian paintings belonging to the same tradition—one by Carpaccio, another by Mantegna, and the third by Bellini—can, with their beauty and their rigor, instruct us. The fact that such works arise out of devotion holds, with regard to sleep, a decisive consequence. There are situations where the sleeping body that is given to us to see as an image is and remains exterior to us, and elicits only our spectatorial pleasure and our admiration for the artistry of the painter. There are others where the representation of cowardice or of betrayal rouses our pity for its victim and our reprobation for the act itself. But the sleep of the apostles at Gethsemane, not wanting to accompany the Word in his fight to give his word to the very end, could not be for us a foreign event that we would consider with detachment or scandal. It concerns our evasion, our withdrawal, our sleep. We see ourselves sleeping when we should be awake. This sleep has something terrible about it, in that we know it to be and recognize it as our own.

Pascal, in *Le mystère de Jésus (The Mystery of Jesus)*, pondered this sleep with incomparable insight: "Jesus seeks companionship and solace from men. It seems to me that this is unique in his whole life, but he finds none, for his disciples are asleep. Jesus will be in agony until the end of the world. There must be no sleeping during that time."[13] And Jesus' prayer in this hour concerns us as well: it delivers us from the despair and opprobrium that our vision of our evasion might bring. As Pascal says further, "Jesus brought about the salvation of his disciples while they slept. He has done this for each of the righteous while they slept, in nothingness before their birth and in their sins after their birth." This sleep does not necessarily presuppose closed eyes, no more than the invitation not to "sleep during that time" advises insomnia.

The seriousness and the gravity of this scene of desertion can be inscribed into the landscape itself. This is what happens in the painting by Carpaccio, which is in Venice. At the summit of a rocky promontory, at the upper left edge of the canvas, Jesus, clothed in red, prays, his hands joined, his head raised toward the sky. On the shelf where he remains, a tree extends its trunk and branches over the void, vainly clawing at the darkness. Everything is naked, desolate, dead. Only stunted bushes in tortured forms pierce the dry ground. We see Jerusalem in the distance and the road that leads there. The nocturnal character of the scene is rendered strongly present. In the foreground, beneath Christ, on two other shelves of rock, as if on a stairway of renunciation, there are the apostles asleep.

The first, following a horizontal line that is directly opposed to the vertical line of Jesus' body, lies upon his belly, his head upon his forearms. The two others form with him a sort of ellipse, following various postures. One still holds a book in his hand, and, his elbow on a rock, supports his head with the other hand. The bodies of the sleepers follow and emphasize the curves of the terrain. They all turn their backs toward Jesus, who stands over and above them. The spiritual separation translates strongly into spatial separation. The apostles form nothing more than clumps of sleep, weighing with all their mass upon the ground. The horizontality of the youngest parodies the liturgical gestures of adoration or of consecration. But he gives himself up to the ground, not to the spirit. The ardent uprightness of Jesus praying invites the thought that he is represented at the moment of accepting the Father's will, rather than at the moment of anguish and of struggle. The dramaturgy of the landscape expresses as much as do the characters the meaning of this dark hour. Nature is also sad unto death here, offering nothing that might appease or gladden the gaze. It is indeed a landscape of dereliction.

The works of Mantegna and of Giovanni Bellini, respectively, are quite different. In Mantegna's painting, space opens and deepens everywhere.[14] The praying Jesus' body does not stand out against the somber background of nearby rock, but instead against the splendid walls of an ideal Jerusalem, and against its proud statuesque mountains. The "rock prie-dieu" or "podium," as Pierre Francastel calls it, is halfway between art and nature: neither an altogether human work, nor an entirely natural place.[15] A few staircase steps separate the shelf where Jesus is from the place where the three apostles sleep. Their abandon, a notable detail, has not made them lose their haloes, which are clearly visible. They seem almost to have been struck down by a sleep that has suddenly made them fall, one upon the other. Two of them have their heads almost touching, propped up by the same rock, and the third has collapsed upon the second, his head resting on the other's thigh. Their open mouths show the depth of their sleep. These heaped-up bodies seem deserted by the spirit.

From the foreground where they are there winds a road on which, farther off, Judas appears, his arm extended, indicating the direction to the soldiers that follow him. The apostles sleep on the road itself, like guards who have fallen asleep, at the foot of the shelf upon which their master prays. And their exceptional sleep is underscored by the very composition of the scene. We seem to be in the morning, and not the night; Johannes Wilde speaks of "bright daylight, when the forms are at their sharpest."[16] Even the most distant sections of the landscape can be seen with a perfect clarity. Rabbits play on the road; pelicans, a christological symbol, float in the water; a bird perched on a tree watches Jesus: it seems that the entire world is wide awake and attends to its tasks, with the sole exception of the apostles. On a cloud, several cherubs show to Jesus a cross and the instruments of the Passion.

Similar to that of his brother-in-law Mantegna, the work of Giovanni Bellini gives even more importance to the landscape.[17] If this painting is admired for its amplitude, its elegance, and its construction,[18] it nevertheless takes away the spiritual intensity and concentration of the scene, casting us too quickly toward dreamy distances. Here again, the sleeping apostles are in the foreground, but, instead of being on the vertical in relation to Jesus, as in the canvases of Carpaccio and of Mantegna, respectively, they form a triangle on his left. No longer grouped but separated, each is in a different position. On the right, the first apostle is lying on his back, with one knee raised; on the left, the second apostle leans with his back against a low wall, his mouth open, head tipped back, and right hand between his knees. At the top of the triangle, the third apostle has crossed his arms on an upright knee and laid his head there. An elegant bridge of stone crosses the stream that separates them from the road upon which, in the distance, soldiers advance. The light is gentle: dawn has broken. High in the sky, a transparent and plump cherub with the wings of a dragonfly shows his chalice to Jesus, who looks intently at him while praying. There is too much grace and too much charm, and too much light, as well, for a lesson in darkness.

What is shown each time in these three paintings is the *depth* of sleep into which the apostles are plunged. It seems so heavy that nothing could draw them out of it. The postures also exhibit fixedness: this is not a momentary drowsiness. But, if one were to isolate these sleepers from the scene in which they figure, nothing would indicate that there is something serious or terrible about this sleep. They seem, by themselves, to sleep the "sleep of the righteous." The Gospel of Luke mentions that the apostles were "sleeping for sorrow."[19] It is hardly visible in these paintings.

It is on the contrary strongly visible in the admirable engraving Dürer devoted to Gethsemane. In the one from the Great Passion woodcuts, the apostles are in the foreground forming the two lower angles of a triangle with Christ as the summit. The apostles' faces are as overwhelmed and tormented as is the landscape itself. As Sophie Renouard de Bussièrre notes: "The sleep of the three disciples has been carefully differentiated according to their age and their temperament: Peter, the oldest, sleeps with his hand closed upon the sword that he will soon employ. James, his chin resting on his hands, seems the prey of dark nightmares. John, in the posture of a melancholic, his face haggard with worry, appears to be dreaming more than sleeping."[20] The engraving emphasizes the overwhelming weight of their heads. The distress that they attempted to flee in sleep has accompanied them there. It is not so much the betrayal of one who isolates himself and withdraws into himself that Dürer displays here, as the weakness for bearing these dark hours. They cannot, or will not be able, to understand that the mystery of the salvation of man is accomplished by the handing over, the suffering, and the passion of Jesus, whom they love. What is foreign to the human view in all of this overwhelms them.

In the same nocturnal and tormented possibility stands the beautiful *Christ in the Olive Garden* by Jordaens.[21] Jesus, in three-quarters view, his arms spread, his hands open, kneeling and braced by an angel whose young face brings out the singularly emaciated, aged, and lined aspects of his face, accepts the Passion, the signs of which are multiple. Usually an angel is represented presenting Jesus with a chalice, but this is sometimes replaced by a cross. Jordaens here figures both. The chiaroscuro burrows into the solitude of the faces and the folds of the clothing. We glimpse the moon behind the leaves in a cloudy sky. In the distance burn the torches of the soldiers who advance, and in the foreground, next to the sleeping Peter is the frail light of a lantern, which no longer has any purpose. It knows better than the apostles how to stay awake. The apostles form a kind of pedestal of sleep for the prayer of Jesus. They are at his feet. Here again the postures are those of dejection and of sorrow. The heads are weighed down, and the best-lit face is hollow and tormented. Hope against all hope forces its painful way, while sleeping humanity is without any resource to free itself from the mounting despair. To grasp what these sleeping bodies bring in their own right to the meaning of the scene, we have only to compare such a work to those in which, as in Veronese,[22] the disciples, set off in the middle ground, form only a secondary element of the painting.

The iconography of sleep runs up against difficulties of another sort when the goal is the evocation of a revelation received in a dream. How can that which the sleeper alone sees and is able to see be shown? The simplest solution, but also the most unsatisfactory, consists in representing in the same space as that of the dreamer what he sees in his dream. This is what happens, for example, in the *Legend of Saint Ursula* by Carpaccio. In her carefully bordered bed-sheets, Ursula sleeps in peace, her cheek nestled against the palm of her hand. In front of her, as if he had just opened the door, an angel, who projects his shadow on the floor of the room, holds the crown of the martyrdom that he announces to her. The light proceeding from the opened door illuminates a small dog lying at the foot of the bed. Without any knowledge of the legend, nothing would allow us to think that the angel appears to the sleeping girl in a dream. The realistic details would have us imagine the contrary: that he is visiting Ursula and is going to wake her. To resolve this difficulty, it is certainly allowable to render the content of the dream vaporous, to bathe it in an unreal light, to represent it otherwise than with a sleeping body, but there always remains a certain uneasiness in front of this type of work. Whence the striking character of Ribera's *Dream of Jacob*.[23]

The simplicity and the s⸳riety of this work, which
ground its greatness, have been rightly praised. As
Jonathan Brown writes, "the composition is daringly
reduced to a simple right angle turned on its side, one arm
of which is formed by the tree stump, the other, by the
slumbering, inert figure of Jacob. His head is illuminated
by a broad beam of light, in the midst of which angels, their
forms so delicately brushed as to be almost invisible,
descend the heavenly ladder."[24] With his left hand, Jacob,
dressed in black, supports his head, seen in three-quarter
view. The white sleeve of his shirt is one of the few light
notes. His other hand rests against the rock. His knees are
drawn up toward his body. Opposed to the darker sky on
the left against which the tree is outlined, a luminous and
golden cloud comes to bless Jacob's body and reveal his
face, deeply absorbed in the dream. To this supernatural
light there responds another that, coming from the left,
causes Jacob's body to project a shadow against the
ground.[25] The nobility of Jacob's face is, in keeping with the
art of Ribera, that of the ordinary and the quotidian. This
naked and simple place in which he has fortuitously, he
believes, lain down in the open to sleep becomes in his
sleep a place of glory and a "gate of heaven." He neither
prepared for nor expected anything—God alone has the
initiative of his revelation.

It is difficult to indicate the ladder of the angels in a more
allusive, discrete, and at the same time sure way than does
Ribera. And it is beautiful that, in the biblical account, what
forms that which Jacob alone can see is, in the painting,
what gives it to us to see. Nothing distinguishes this sleeping body from another, except that it appears bathed in the
brightness of its own dream. Rembrandt, in some of his
drawings, was similarly modest, yet, while he does not
show the ladder, he does make an angel appear before the
sleeping Jacob. What is it about such a sleep that transfig-
ures and illuminates the body? God can work even though
we sleep, and God can enter into relations with us even

though we have temporarily suspended our life of relation—his word can reach us even though we no longer
answer for or to anything. The sleeping bodies of the apostles on the Mount of Olives are bodies that can no longer
face up to what comes, or bear it; they are bodies that can
no longer receive. Here, the body of Jacob is the site of
receptivity. Its passivity makes it the receptacle of the
divine manifestation. God can come to find us even in our
innermost moments, without our having searched for or
called to him. To this peaceful sleep—it is only when he
awakes that Jacob becomes afraid, taking account of the
exceptional nature of the place where he slept—is opposed
another biblical slumber, that of Noah. It puts into play the
shameful nudity of the father fallen asleep drunk, and the
respect or disrespect of the sons.

It is certainly more rarely evoked by painting than
other slumbers. And indeed, the plastic evocation of this
episode is caught by definition in an insurmountable paradox. The object of the account, which furnishes the
motive for the curse set upon Ham and his descendants,
is to oppose the filial disrespect of Ham, who looked upon
the nudity of his father, and, according to the tradition,
mocked him, to the respect of Shem and Japheth who "took
a garment, laid it upon both their shoulders, and walked
backward and covered the nakedness of their father; their
faces were turned away, and they did not see their father's
nakedness."[26] Any illustration of the account, then, makes
new Hams of us, because this forbidden nudity is precisely
given to see to teach us the interdiction. To take into consideration Shem and Japheth who turn away, we have to
look directly at that away from which they turn. It is true
that, for Christians,[27] this scene forms the prefiguration of
the mocking of Christ stripped bare, a scene of outrage, just
as Noah in a general way refers to the Christ to come and
to his ark the Church. What is more, this drunkeness, the
first in history, follows the very first vintage, and Noah's
fault is involuntary. But this does not prevent the paradox

from remaining. Unless one holds to the evangelical dispo-
sition according to which "to the pure, everything is pure,"
the representation of this drunkeness seems to have the
structure of a "double bind." To this spiritual paradox
there is sometimes added another. Certain sculptors, such
as Baccio Bandinelli,[28] or painters, such as Michelangelo in
the Sistine Chapel, show the sons of Noah completely
naked in front of their father, as if in a mythological scene.
The scene, which, far from being situated in a palaestra,
rests entirely on the revealing of what is not to be shown,
thus becomes absurd and incomprehensible.

Pictorial art of the high Middle Ages confronted this
episode, since it is present in the wall paintings of the
abbey of Saint-Savin-sur-Gartempe, one of the masterpieces of the Romanesque style. Henri Focillon describes
the work in the following way: Noah "lying on the ground,
leaves open to view, between the flaps of his half-open
frock coat, his terrible nudity, streaked white and red. One
would say that it is made of strips of leather and dowels of
wood. The good sons make ready to throw a veil over the
shame of their father, which a group of women looks upon
with disgust."[29] It is necessary to add that the mockery here
is much stronger than in later works, for Ham, on the left,
makes an obscene gesture with his right hand in the direction of the body of the sleeping Noah. This theme of humil-
iated sleep is taken up again during the Renaissance in an
impressive work by Giovanni Bellini.[30] According to
Millard Meiss, it is "the first independent representation,
outside of a biblical cycle, of *The Drunkeness of Noah.*"

The naked and slender body of Noah extends, in a posture of abandon, to the full length of the foreground of the
painting, as if thrown into view, the left hand on his shoulder, the right arm lying above his lined and hoary head,
legs spread apart, like a faun; a flap of a cloak, which Shem
and Japheth, eyes turned aside, delicately begin to place
upon him, is already covering his sex. A bunch of grapes is
evident to the left of his distorted face. The two respectful

sons are situated on either side of him, while the crude-looking, sneering face of Ham lies above him, in the center of the painting. With his two hands he makes a gesture as if to prevent his brothers from veiling their father's body. Space is completely obturated, leaving us no place where we can turn our eyes. As Michel Laclotte notes, Bellini "limits the field of vision to the figures, without any space above or below, blocked by a tight curtain of vines."[31] Johannes Wilde speaks rightly of "brutality" and of an "extraordinary expressive power."[32]

This obscene sleep is like the antithesis of all the erotic sleeping nudities that begin to multiply at the same time and in the same places. Here, sleep reveals a fragility of the human body abandoned, offered, and exposed without measure to the gaze and the mockery of others, deprived of any possibility of withdrawal or resistance. It is the body of a victim. Not the victim of an act of violence, but of a gaze that causes shame. To have been, without knowing it and despite oneself, an object of mockery for others is the extremity of shame. This is why there is also violence in such a representation, which is properly considered obscene. And at the same time, it juxtaposes the two possibilities open to us in front of this exposition of a defenseless body: that of a sense of decency, which does not want to see anything that the other did not want to show, a filiality that can be universalized, in which the sons become themselves paternal with regard to the father delivered up to outrage; or the complete opposite possibility of a mockery that causes shame, and spreads it. The Scriptures do not say that Ham made fun of his father, but that instead of covering him he went immediately to fetch his brothers. To fall asleep is for all intents and purposes to deliver oneself up to others. But this delivery can also be a way to rely upon the other, for example, to rely upon his respect, a respect all the more great in that we are precisely no longer in a position to command it or to make it prevail. The nudity of man is one, here, with his fragility, but also with trust.

The gospel scene of the calmed storm[33] puts another
slumber into play, with completely different tensions, and
a different trust. Jesus falls asleep peacefully and continues
to sleep while the boat in which he sails with the apostles
is overtaken by a sudden storm. Afraid, the apostles wake
him. After having calmed the wind and the water through
the sole power of his words, Jesus questions his companions about their faith. And they pass from one fear to
another, from the fear of dying to the reverential fear
elicited by the miracle of the elements' irresistible obedience to the words of Jesus. Here it is Jesus who sleeps amid
the breaking waves, and, in their panic, the apostles take
this sleep as a sort of indifference to their fate, a sort of
abandonment. While this sleep has inspired numerous
meditations by the Church Fathers and the Christian tradition, from Saint Ambrose of Milan and Saint Augustine[34] to
the phrase of Pascal: "There is some pleasure in being on
board a ship battered by storms when one is certain of not
perishing,"[35] it is by contrast little present in painting. And
yet the dramatic character of the scene would seem to lend
itself to pictorial evocation. But this relative abstention
doubtless has plastic grounds. Indeed, to show a man
calmly dozing amidst the greatest peril would place us in
the very situation of the apostles: "Teacher, do you not care
if we perish?"[36] This vision would suggest thoughtlessness,
obliviousness, indifference. How does one show plastically
that the heart of Jesus watches while he sleeps, that he still
remains, even asleep, the Lord, and that he has not
deserted the situation? How does one avoid looking upon
this slumber with an unbelieving gaze, the gaze that Jesus
reproves to his companions?

Rembrandt, in an early work,[37] took another tack, which
avoids this aporia: he caught Jesus at the very moment when
the disciples have come to wake him. The irresistible whiteness of a wave powerfully raises the prow of the boat, and
pours into it dangerously. The threatened cross of the mast
glistening in the storm, strongly inclined, distinguishes by

its diagonal two groups of apostles. One group, underlined with foam, fusses powerlessly about the mast and the rigging; the others, surrounding Jesus, shout to him their distress and their anguish. Among these, one still has a hand placed upon Jesus, as if to urge him to act. Another, seen from the back, seems exhausted, while yet another, sick, bends over the water. Far from this critical tension, where the anguish takes all sorts of forms without ceasing to be the same disarray, the calm of Jesus lying down ballasts the boat in peril and already announces the words that he will utter, or rather exercise.

Delacroix was haunted by this slumber of Jesus during the storm. In 1853 and 1854, he painted a dozen works inspired by this scene, *Le Christ sur le lac de Génésareth*.[38] They are distinguishable from one another above all by the orientation and nature of the boat, sometimes a rowboat, sometimes a sailboat. These strongly romantic paintings make us hear the silence of the Word sleeping amidst the cries of men and the sounds of the waves. To underline the meaning of the scene, Delacroix had recourse to the conventional solution that consists in haloing, supernaturally, the face of the sleeping Jesus. This certainly isolates him from the surrounding agitation, and sets him apart, but this almost ecstatic sleep loses at the same time some of its reality. It is a poem about the stormy sea, the contemplation of which (at Dieppe) was then fascinating the painter, as much as or perhaps even more than it is a meditation upon sleep. Jesus here seems above the human and natural fray. The Church Fathers saw in the slumber on the boat the attestation of Jesus' full humanity, just as in the miracle of the calming of the storm they saw the attestation of his full divinity. For Delacroix, Jesus sleeps a sleep that is perhaps too divine. There remains the jewel of this silence within the thick gangue of tumult.

This eloquent silence can serve as both conclusion and criteria. The human body still carries speech even when in sleep it is quiet. In falling asleep, the body deserts neither the word nor the spirit—it does not become an uninhabited body. It still and always delivers trust or anguish, doubt or peace. This is why there is a plurality of sleep, which painting enumerates in its polyptychs, and not a return to the undifferentiated. Never will we be able to stop witnessing, to cease being those who carry the word with their whole body. The preface to all speech, the breath of our breathing, is the first act of presence, that which is interrupted only with the interruption of life itself. Yet, if the body while sleeping does not lose its glimmer, this glimmer remains the glimmer of its secret. It is to this secret that our gaze responds, and must respond. Far from spreading itself out before my eyes like a spectacle that I might scrutinize and autopsy, the sleeping body is something to which, following Claudel's expression, the eye listens.

The secret eloquence of this silence, which both entrusts speech to me and entrusts itself to my speech, serves also as a criteria. The multiple sleeping nudes that painting gives us to see stage the fantasy of an integral visibility, of a body passively delivered over to a gaze, of a body without protection, but also of a body removed from speech, and thus, in its insignificance, perfectly masterable. It tends to lose its face, as in Eustache Le Sueur's *Vénus endormie surprise par l'Amour (Sleeping Venus Surprised by Love),* where the woman's body is offered in full light, while her face avoids notice in the shadows.[39] Let us leave these bodies where they are, for they do nothing more, precisely, than be there in the imaginary—they do not exist. They would call for the same complacency as that with which they are incessantly shown. Let's allow them to lose speech. And let's breathe a bit.

NOTES

1. Proust, *A la recherche du temps perdu,* t. III, 579; tran. Moncrieff, *Remembrance of Things Past,* 2:426–27.

2. Proust, *A la recherche,* 581; tran. Moncrieff, *Remembrance,* 428.

3. Gen. 28:10–19.
4. I Kings 3:4–15.
5. Matt. 1:19–25.
6. Gen. 9:20–27.
7. Matt. 8:23–27.
8. Matt. 26:36–46.
9. Cf. Meiss, "Sleep in Venice," 212–39.
10. Cf. Forestier, Sérullaz, and Sérullaz, *Delacroix*, 15–16, 22–23, 30, 66–67.
11. Andujar, Budapest, Buenos Aires.
12. Toledo (Ohio), London, Bilbao.
13. Pascal, *Pensées*, Brunschvicg §553, Lafuma §919; tran. Krailsheimer, 289; see 290 for the following quotation.
14. National Gallery, London.
15. Francastel, *La figure et le lieu*, 294.
16. Wilde, *Venetian Art*, 4. Cf. 4, on the other version Mantegna painted of this scene (at Tours).
17. National Gallery, London.
18. Cf. Wilde, *Venetian Art*, 4, 9; and Humfrey, *Painting in Renaissance Venice*, 63–64.
19. Luke 22:45
20. Bussièrre, *Albrecht Dürer*, 108.
21. Honfleur. Cf. the commentary by J. Foucart and J. Lacambre, in Bruyn, *Le siècle de Rubens*, 116–17.
22. Milan.
23. Prado, Madrid.
24. Brown, *Golden Age of Painting*, 190.
25. Cf. the commentary by D. M. Pagano, in Ascione, *La pittura napoletana dal Caravaggio*, 250.
26. Gen. 9:23.
27. Meiss, "Sleep in Venice," 226; and Laclotte, *Le siècle de Titien*, 270–71.
28. Florence, cf. Meiss, "Sleep in Venice," 350.
29. Focillon, *Peintures romanes des églises*, 51.
30. *The Drunkeness of Noah*, Besançon.
31. Laclotte, *Le siècle de Titien*, 271.
32. Wilde, "Sleep in Venice," 69.
33. In addition to Matt. 8:23–27, cf. Mark 4:35–41, Luke 8:22–25.
34. La Bonnardière, "La tempête apaisée," 145–48.

35. Pascal, *Pensées*, Brunschvicg §859; Lafuma §743; tran. Krailsheimer, 229.
36. Mark 4:38.
37. 1633, Boston.
38. Cf. Forestier, Sérullaz, and Sérullaz, *Delacroix*, 24–25.
39. San Francisco. Cf. Rosenberg, *La peinture française du XVIIe siècle*, 271.

The Strange Beauty
of Charon

THE STRANGE BEAUTY of Charon is that which, in magnifying him, is conferred upon him by Pierre Subleyras' painting from the first half of the eighteenth century, itself strange and beautiful, entitled *Charon passant les ombres sur le Styx*, in the Louvre. Strange indeed is this splendid and radiant nude, which makes the figure usually depicted by mythology as a hideous old man appear like a young athlete. In the sixth song of the *Aeneid*, Virgil exposes Charon's powerful horror, as if the pilot of the infernal rivers, in his inexorable abandon, could only himself be infernal too:

> Grim Charon is the squalid ferryman,
> is guardian of these streams, these rivers; his
> white hairs lie thick, disheveled on his chin;
> his eyes are fires that stare, a filthy mantle
> hangs down his shoulder by a knot. Alone,
> he poles the boat and tends the sails and carries
> the dead in his dark ship, old as he is;
> but old age in a god is tough and green.[1]

Even more than painting, poetry has let itself be haunted by this ultimate crossing, this passing within the passing, and by its harsh ferryman, sometimes in order to turn our attention away from this haunting obsession. Thus Ronsard, in his *Hymne de la mort*, writes:

> Tu me diras encore que tu trambles de crainte
> D'un batelier Charon, qui passe par contrainte
> Les ames outre l'eau d'un torrent effroyant

> You will tell me again how you tremble with fear
> At a ferryman named Charon, who by force leads
> Souls across the water of a terrifying torrent

before dismissing this anguish that makes us "like children" by recalling the sacrifice of Christ on the cross.[7] Neither Charon nor anyone else makes Baudelaire's "Don Juan in Hell" give up his impenitent impassibility. Charon passes, too, from one poetry to another.

When this crossing was painted, as in the *Passage du Styx* by Joachim Patinir, which is in the Prado, Charon figured very much as one would expect: a resolved old man, whom the painter renders gigantic in the eyes of the single soul, who is terrified, frail, lonely, and trembling in the prow of the boat. Charon transports the soul with a sort of impatience, his haste fluttering and lifting the linen that clothes him. Pushing on his boathook, majestically centered in an immense landscape, he figures the irreparable. Beyond the indistinct entrance to Hell glow cities in flames, like Sodoms and Gomorrahs from beyond the grave, endlessly consumed.

Completely different is the Charon depicted by Subleyras, who breaks with the mythological and iconographic tradition. No longer do we perceive the fatal boat, as in the painting by Patinir, with a commanding eagle's eye view. We are there, we ourselves are embarked, and Charon, whose taut imperious body occupies the full vertical range of the painting, is in our proximity as if right before our eyes. The brightness around him of the glowing fires of Hell responds to the rosy tint, here and there, of his skin: it haloes and sculpts its nudity, and exalts the muscular and definitional curves of its contours. Young, powerful, and lively, he is seen from the back, his left knee propped against the gunwale of his boat, the occasion for a fine foreshortening, and the right foot thrust toward the exterior, the entire body buttressed, striving with his tall, knotty, sylvan boathook. The inclination of his torso to the left creases his waist, and his right arm, heavy with swelled muscles, rises to grip the wood well above his head. It is he who gives the painting all its movement. The calm and profound effort of his gesture, in a light that is as precise as it is unreal, offers to his nudity this carnal, dynamic, and taut magnificence, which contrasts strongly with the often cold beauty of Subleyras' other works. His innermost strength vibrates at the very surface of his skin.

But Charon is not alone, he is transporting souls to the place of their greatest distress. These "souls" are only empty clothes, white draperies with a thousand clever folds formed around nothing. Ample hoods hide their absent faces. It would certainly be permissible to say that, in doing so, Subleyras has combined in the same painting two academic studies, the nude and drapery.[3] But this conjunction lends the painting its proper uneasiness, intertwining absence and sensuality. With the head bent in a posture as meditative as it is overwhelmed, and the astonishingly solar body of Charon transfigured through and through, these phantoms of labyrinthine whiteness underscore his living weight.

In this painting without a face, since his is turned away and those of the "souls" have disappeared, Charon is no longer a power of death, the infernal ferryman of Hell, the one who steers there while already showing in his features its imperturbable horror; rather, he forms the ultimate and marvelous luminescence of the life that has been abandoned, of a beauty and youth left on the other bank of time. In his very presence he makes former days felt, and the life that has been lost. The singular chiasmus of these clothes without bodies and this glorious nudity that, like nudes of mythology, does not even seem unclothed, lightens and raises the weight of Charon, a candle of flesh more blazing than the flames, just as it weighs down the "boneless phantoms," encircled by the folds of their own despair. And yet something in this symmetry is unbalanced, and leans like the young man's body. What?

This body so keenly erect, radiating its strength, drives its boathook into the depths of the Styx. To the right, on the final shore, two "souls" pensively consider this new arrival to the kingdom of vain tears and unheard cries. In the background we notice a naked body, tortured, tied to a wheel and turning in the blaze whose ... y glow makes Charon's beauty shine forth. A bat, foreshadowing Goya, flies in the sooty air. The surrection of this body is the contrary of the resurrection: it subtracts from all hope, and its verticality steers its woeful passengers within the horizontal. Why give it this strange beauty, over which no one in this place may rejoice? Why by surprise seem to place us on this fatal boat? Why present so much evidence in what nevertheless remains enigmatic? We have to let the boat go, let this sunflower of flames blossom, and return to the daylight.

Notes

1. Virgil, *Aeneid*, VI, lines 298–304; tran. Mandelbaum *The Aeneid of Virgil*, 148–49.

2. Ronsard, *Hymne de la mort*, lines 183–85 and 197–202, in *Œuvres complètes*, t. VIII, 172.

3. Cf. the note by Michel and Rosenberg, *Subleyras*, 162.

The Cat as
Instrument of Nudity

TO GIVE NUDITY to be seen, it is not enough simply to show a body without clothes. It is necessary to show the absence of clothes, the unclothed or denuded being of the body, and to render present the act in which this body exposes itself. Thus there is always something oblique in any nude that is not merely academic. The nudity of the self is not self-evident. Huysmans, in his writings on art, pointed this out, against the artificial convention of a mythological nudity that tries to pass as natural.[1] Moreover, for there to be true nudity, instruments of nudity are required that recall the denuding that grounds the nude. The simplest and most common such instrument is nothing other than the piece of clothing itself, the item that has been removed. It indexes the nude as such. A fine *Nu au divan* by Caillebotte arranges the model's clothes next to him, and, on the floor, in the foreground, his boots. The presence of clothed bodies next to the denuded body forms only one variant on this first possibility. Manet's *Le dejeuner sur l'herbe* is one of the most notable examples. By their richness, their texture, and their shimmer, fabrics, even if they are not clothes, fulfill the same function, according to which a nude indoors is always more nude than a bather stepping out of the water in nature. But there are more subtle, softer instruments of nudity than clothing and all that which directly evokes clothing. The cat is one. Several paintings make use of the cat in this manner.

First and foremost is Manet's *Olympia*, quickly transformed from an object of scandal into a paradigm of the modern nude through an inversion of the sign of its deviation.

The abundance and thoroughness of commentary elicited by this painting discourages the addition of anything more than an indirect and feline scholium. That which tells of nothing, or almost nothing, calls for narratives. The shameless and sinuous nudity of Olympia ends, indeed, in a playful slipper, nonchalantly directed toward a question mark and an exclamation point that is at once both surprised and fearful, and firmly established on its paws; indeed, toward a black bristlebrush with yellow eyes, which turns out to be a cat. Such a conclusion is perplexing. Théophile Gautier was speechless in front of this "black cat that leaves the imprint of his muddy paws on the bed," though, to tell the truth, our gaze searches in vain for such tracks.[2] Concerning this cat, as well as the painting in its entirety, Georges Bataille carefully described the transformation accomplished by Manet with regard to Titian's *Venus of Urbin*, which *Olympia* translates, before itself being translated by Cézanne in his *Une moderne Olympia*. Bataille writes that, like Olympia herself, who "awakens with a start to this world" and sits up, "the dog lying curled at the edge of the bed has itself stood up: the dog, in this movement, has changed itself into a black cat."[3] In this black cat Bataille sees "the depth of shadow."[4]

In a book that constantly reties *The Ribbon Around the Neck of Olympia* (*Le ruban au cou d'Olympia*), Michel Leiris will make this cat the intermittent guide of an erotic reverie in which the frail young animal becomes by turns "the obscurity of a mystery that allows itself to be touched, yet will not be reduced by any caress," a "household genie or infernal fiend" full of expectation, a "substitute" for that which Olympia's hand hides from our gaze, or the incarnation of an evanescent ineffable. . . .[5] This is a lot, indeed, too much, for a kitten, despite his eyes of gold. This cat's blackness does not render him any darker than does the whiteness of Olympia attest to her candor. Cézanne does not see so much malice here: in his *Modern Olympia* he simply makes the cat disappear, and the client enter. The feline is the sole innocent in this painting. Is he indeed a cat of Egyptian sumptuousness, or of Baudelairean eroticism? The astonishment of the animal with the wide open eyes has nothing metaphysical about it, and was put there by Manet, it seems, not without some humor. The cat has something a bit naïve about it, in a painting that is clearly not so; it is a cat that is almost a child, a cat that is a cat, its own ideogram.

A better tack is to begin with the cat's gaze; Leiris asks, "Mustn't the scene have a witness, just as the painting will have its spectator?"[6] But the cat is not witness to the scene that we see; rather, it has turned toward the client, toward the painter, or toward us. Its movement forms the sign of an irruption in this scene full of immobility. We are caught, while the black servant attentively looks to Olympia, under the crossed and in every sense opposed fire of the eyes of Olympia and the eyes of the cat. Assuredly, this painting draws stares that are no less astonished than those it depicts.

Following the body of Olympia, the gaze does not finally lose itself in the undetermined, but runs up against this quivering wall of fur, and, perhaps, bounces back gently. Its laughable verticality balances the painting. And its multiform antithesis in relation to Olympia, as much by color as by position or expression, certainly sends us back incessantly to her: it is she that it reveals. The cat is the ultimate instrument of nudity in a canvas that contains so many— indeed, a canvas that contains practically all those that could be imagined, from the ribbon to the bracelet to the slipper, from fabrics to the presence of an amply clothed body. Ultimate, and seemingly completely surprised to be so, and to be there.

Let's leave the cat to bristle, and seek out a bit of tranquility from a rounder cat, a cat that has curled up. There is one particularly at its ease in Renoir's *Le jeune garçon au chat*. This carefully composed canvas has the cold perfection of the imaginary. It lives on a haunted absence and a mute premonition. The end of childhood has its troubles that it cannot tell, for, still being childhood, it does not know how to say them, and afterwards it is too late: our words, heavy with tribulations, would tear the fine fabric of rosy innocence, destroying what it was before coming to know it. Kierkegaard, in *The Concept of Anxiety,* has described better than anyone this sheen of ignorance, of "the mind in the state of reverie." In Renoir's painting, the heavy and somber gaze, as if overflowing with dreams, of this boy with feminine lashes and eyes still heavy with rings of sleep, knows much already about what it is not to know. He is perfectly elsewhere in being totally here, in this scene that is nowhere. Clothed only by the bracelet of fur round his left wrist made by the paw and tail of a cat that he encloses in his slender arms, and that clasps him in its own way, his flesh is flat, cold, hairless, pale, with a paleness that, in its slightly bluish cast, is almost disturbing. He is naked, in a posture of feigned spontaneity, as if his body had never come into the light. The union of this slender nudity's dull extinction and extreme exposition is wrenched from an affectionate and bountiful environment.

This body so white, revived only by the pink of his lips, stretches its languor amidst a carnival of fabrics. The wool of a carpet flourishing at his feet, sumptuous white silk sprinkled with blue bouquets and bordered with red, the green velvet of the cushion upon which the cat spreads its fur fluffed out by caresses—so many voluptuous materials for a painting that one would want to see as innocent! The black of the indeterminate background, at the same time in which it grazes the undulating right flank of the boy with a finger of shadow, brings out the sensuality of these fabrics of a rich interiority, supported by some unknown piece of furniture. The voluptuousness of the movements of envelopment and clasping responds to the voluptuousness of the materials. The boy crosses his legs, which makes his hips stick out in an equivocal pose, and, planted on his right foot, he only touches the carpet with the toes of his left foot. Leaning to the left, he places his elbow on an upper

cushion, his head bent close to that of the cat that has seemingly dissolved into quivers and purrings, and his hands
clasp themselves around the back of the animal with its
eyes half-closed. All the curves of his nude body converge
and complete themselves in this dreamy embrace, in an
impossible, artificial, and cold light. The weighty silky fabric that brushes against the young man, which is perhaps in
its ingratiating and feline suppleness the second cat in the
painting, spreads down to the floor, where its double red
border curves and gives a bit of mobility to the painting.
This corolla of corollas seems ready to close and envelope
this languorous nudity.

This painting by Renoir has sometimes been compared
to Parmigianino's *Cupid Sharpening His Bow*.[7] The posture
and the general line of the body are indeed almost identical. But a host of features separate the two canvases, in a
chiasmus that indeed justifies the comparison! Parmesan's
Eros has a body that is much more fleshy and less childish,
which permits him to trim his bow powerfully, with a vigorous knife. Rather doubtful wings, like add-ons, are
grafted onto his shoulders, while his face—graceful, completely pink, and truly puerile—has little harmony with the
rest of his body. Half pensive, half resolute, he looks
toward the virtual spectator. This playful allegory, which
contains more than one amusing detail, has nothing unsettling about it. Renoir's boy, in taking on a more delicate
body, has lost his wings and no longer looks anywhere but
into the spirals of his caressed and caressing daydream.

And above all, he has entered into the unsettling order,
which painting once cherished, of nudity amidst the profusion of fabrics. The cat here, as in *Olympia*, is only one
instrument of nudity among others. The entire staging—
for this is assuredly staged—lays bare to the point of
shamelessness, and gives the impression of déjà vu that all
of the devices of denudation have. Far from merely under-
lining by its fur the skin's nudity, the cat here forms the key
to a transparent enigma, it incarnates metonymically the

caress wandering and diffused throughout the entire painting. A scene of insatisfaction can only imagine the curled up plenitude of a feline vibrating with comfort. This is not the exclamatory cat of *Olympia*.

More overtly unsettling is the scene of entrapment constructed by Balthus in his *Le Lever (The Waking Up)*.[8] A naked young girl, whose left foot alone is hidden from view by the covers pushed down to the end of her bed, uses a game to prolong the liveliness and instantaneousness usually evoked by the leap from bed. With her right foot barely resting on the ground, and opening her prepubescent thighs, she stares intently with her black and almost Asiatic eyes, her lips wrinkled by mischievous malice, at the mechanical bird that her long and slender fingers hold by the foot, as if in the moment of taking flight. The bird has an Easter-egg body, as if proud of being so blue, which is surmounted by two wings fringed with red, the narrow base of which has a questionable power of support; and above all there is a protruding, immense eye, also blue with a black pupil, the eye of a nightmare insect that looks at us without seeing, disconcerted by absence, and by having before it only a tiny red beak. This impossible toy flowering at the fingertips of the girl possesses for the cat with yellow eyes slashed with black, emerging from one of those baskets that serve to transport his like during a trip, an entirely other power of fascination than for us, since it is properly speaking hallucinated. The soft diagonal line of the girl's flank, extending across the bed, is doubled by a diagonal line of lure and inveiglement, setting out on the same axis the playful eyes of the awakened beauty, the mad eyes of the unreal bird, the girl's other, empty hand inviting the bird to take flight, and the eyes of the liberated cat, heavy with an impending sudden bound, promising paws and claws.

The vibrant porosity of surfaces, the texture of materials that is at once both vaporous and precise, and the softness of the light give an intense sensuality to the canvas. This cat is doubtless a dummy, according to more than one meaning, and what you see may not be what you get.[9] That he comes out of his basket at the same time that the girl emerges from her covers, where the covers and the basket are significantly both gathered at the bottom of the bed, clearly makes of his fur the revelation of her skin, an index of human nudity. But that he comes out only to enter into another form of trap—the winged lure flapping at the fingertips of the shameless Alice—is nevertheless cause for anxiety. For this lure hides and manifests another, of which it is only a cog: that of the painting itself. Is this cat, haunted by the unreal and captivated by a staging, not the spectator's lieutenant, his ambassador inside the phantasm? Without all of these gazes, would we have the same ease in allowing our own gaze to linger? Indeed, who precisely is outwitted by the unassailable that exposes itself here? An acid sharpness lives at the heart of all of this sweetness, and at the heart of this trap designed to render the gaze voyeuristic. Already in Balthus's *La chambre* a hieratic cat watched the angular dwarf who watched the sleeping beauty suddenly denuded by the irruption of light.

Such nudes thus implemented using fur are neither the first, nor the last. There is, for instance, a seventeenth-century *Boy with Cat* by Giovanni Lanfranco. Naked upon a bed with wrinkled sheets, obliquely struck by a vivid light that deepens shadows and underscores relief, a young man, viewed at three-quarters and from the back, leans, half straightened, with his left elbow on an embroidered cushion, while his right arm stretches slowly to pet a cat hungry for yet more caresses. The cat, placing its paws on his thigh, looks at his delicate face framed by long hair, as if to draw up close. A turned-down sheet, which unfolds in waves to the foreground of the painting, covers what must be covered. This peaceful nudity beats with a rhythm of diagonal lines, concluded by the parted legs of the boy: to the movement of his right arm stretched out toward the cat, profiled against a heavy curtain that serves as backdrop, there responds the forward protrusion of his right leg bent back toward the lower extremity of the canvas. An inverse symmetry is formed by his left foot and elbow. But, above his shoulder, the young coaxer gazes smiling toward the spectator. This would be merely a nice academic nude but for this cat, and this play of gazes, these drapes, and the undulations of light and of fabric. Indeed, the nineteenth century did not discover the cat as instrument of nudity.

Do such cats exist only in painting? At the beginning of Alfred de Musset's libertine, humorous, and chatty *Conte oriental* entitled *Namouna* (which literary historians tell us was produced as evidence by the lawyer defending Baudelaire at his trial for the *Fleurs du mal* to serve as precedent to "Les Bijoux"), the poet devotes several stanzas to the nudity of his character—a nudity, however, that is never actually described.[10] He only names it, over and over again. Of Hassan, who is lying upon a sofa "of bearskin," which is nonetheless "velvety like a cat and fresh like a rose," all decidedly too much for a bearskin, it is said (and this concludes the first sextain) that "He was as naked as Eve at her first sin."

And, as if the inversion of the common figure—as naked as Adam—were not enough, Musset will strike the drum of his comparisons again and again. "Hassan was thus naked,—as naked as a hand,—/As naked as a silver platter,—as naked as a church wall,/As naked as an academician's speech." This "as naked as," driven to the point of burlesque, is an instrument of nudity. It lives off of a fundamental paradox: only the human body is and may be naked, and human nudity is thus precisely *like* nothing else—like nothing other than itself. One can only be naked like a man. "As naked as a hand" only confirms this.[11] Every comparison bearing on nudity only masks it and weakens it, instead of illuminating it. Here the words *like* or *as* are always an accent, authorizing the repetition of the word *naked*. And it is indeed thus that Musset understands the word, as he introduces the reader, and especially the female reader, into his description, as if we were included in the scene.

The listing and the description of instruments of nudity according to their various classes would be long. What should we retain from this panoply, the purpose of which is sufficiently indicated by a cat? Is it not the case that the misunderstanding of nudity as an action goes hand in hand with the imaginary fascination for a nudity that never appears nude enough, which must always be denuded further, and the deployment of so many oblique resources to uncover the uncovering? When it is not mere undressing, when it truly takes place, it is someone who attests to himself or herself as exposed presence, a presence that does no more than come before our own presence, and not solely before our eyes, without such a coming, along with everything about it that is unimaginable, ceasing to come about unexpectedly.

The event of nudity is not implemented. It is that to which all instrumentation, employed to capture it, will in advance be blinded.

NOTES

1. See my study, "L'âme nue," in La voix nue, 31–60.

2. Quoted by Bataille, *Manet*, 57; tran. Wainhouse and Emmons, 62 [translation modified].

3. Bataille, *Manet*, 64; tran. Wainhouse and Emmons, 69 [translation modified].

4. Bataille, *Manet*, 68; tran. Wainhouse and Emmons, 70–71.

5. Leiris, *Le ruban au cou d'Olympia*, 70, 122, 150, 208, respectively.

6. Ibid., 122.

7. Cf. the account devoted to this painting by Loyrette, *Impressionnisme: les origines, 1589–1869*, 453.

8. Cf. Leymarie, *Balthus*, 104–5. Balthus's oeuvre contains several other nudes with cat.

9. Translator's note: The French reads, *"Ce chat est fourré."* *Fourré* here means covered with fur, as well as stuffed and deceitfully dressed-up or covered over.

10. Musset, *Poésies complètes*, 239–40, and the note 697–98.

11. Translator's note: The expression *"nu comme la main"* is akin to English expressions like "as naked as the day he was born."

From God the Artist to Man the Creator

HOW DID THE CREATOR become an artist? How did the artist become a creator? Put another way, how did the creative act, which for the biblical Revelation properly belongs only to God, come to be thought of thanks to schemas borrowed from the properly human act of production and of fabrication? And how did the human producer come to designate himself by the divine name of creator? Through a strange exchange, with measureless consequences for the history of art, a human model was transferred to God, and a divine model to man. What was gained and what was lost in such an exchange? What was its price, which we perhaps continue to pay in multiple ways? That this exchange may for us be obscured by the very familiarity of its effects only makes it more worthy of being elucidated, and of being traced back to the decisions by which it was brought about. Without thinking of where it comes from, current language indeed speaks of literary, pictorial, or musical "creation," as well as "creation" in more frivolous domains. The modern opposition of the artist and the craftsman often appeals to this thinking: in its uniqueness and radical newness, the work of art is to be deemed a creation, while the product of handicraft, applying preestablished rules and preexisting models, is not to be named with this name. More recently, the handicrafts have taken up this opposition for their own benefit, in order to distinguish themselves from industrial production. Who made these now familiar words possible?

How did the creator become an artist? How did the artist become a creator? Without being identical or constituting the same history, these two questions nonetheless form a whole. Once God is thought of as the supreme artist, it is inevitable that one would come to place the artist as a being within God's divine order, and make the artist's power to produce new forms a reflection of the power of God. And it is no less inevitable, even if only at the endpoint, that the artist would separate himself from other producers by the fact of taking himself for a creator, a god among men. This process took time, and required many decisions. But it is clear that the first, inaugural decision concerns the thinking of divine creation itself as art. Without that, the other decision would not have had any ground to stand on, truly or durably. In order for this history to be a serious one, as it is, it must also be a theological history. Indeed, only a theology could name God as artist in a manner that would make this name, even new, remain with him. And likewise, only a theology could name man as creator in a way that this name, even improbable, would keep its weight and, little by little, impose itself. It remains to show that this was indeed the case. That this history is theological does not signify that it must remain so, nor that once these decisions were made they might not reign outside of the space in which they were taken, or even against it.

This history does not begin without a powerful strangeness, for it brings together two traditions that seemed unlikely to cross in such a place. All of the terms through which we think about art, at least the original terms, are of Greek provenance: they were formed independently of any idea of creation, for the ancient Greeks, not imagining even the possibility that the world had been created out of nothing, could not in any way compare the activity of the artist to that of God calling things into being solely through his speech. As for the Bible, it does not describe the divine creation through an artistic analogy. Nevertheless, if to create is proper to God, and is distinguished from all human production that transforms matter, it sometimes happens that the Bible compares God to a craftsman, as in the case of the book of Isaiah: "Shall the potter be regarded as the clay; that the thing made should say of its maker, 'He did not make me,' and a pot say to its potter, 'He has no understanding'?"[1] But the aim of such comparisons is not to illuminate the nature of divine operations, nor to study any sort of divine art: they simply underscore the radical dependence of the creature upon the creator. That God in the *Letter to the Hebrews* is named the craftsman (*tekhnitès*) of the city hoped for by Abraham displays the special holiness of Jerusalem; the text does not specify what the creative act is.[2] Thus production was thought of without creation, and creation, unless in analogies of power and of mastery, was thought of without production, for it acts through speech alone.

The encounter of these two concepts could not fail to modify profoundly their respective economy and understanding. The weight of the question only becomes more serious if we take account of the fact that, in Greek philosophy, the study of *tekhnè* and of *poièsis,* of art and of production, understood each in the broadest sense, hardly constitutes a secondary or regional problem. Heidegger said it powerfully: "Not only did the Greeks, Plato and Aristotle, carry out the interpretation of this phenomenon of production, but the basic concepts of philosophy have grown out of and within this interpretation."[3] Greek thinking about art is characterized by two features: art is a *know-how (un savoir-faire),* and it is the *making of a work (un faire œuvre).* A knowledge of making is first of all a knowledge and, as such, essentially communicable and teachable: that which cannot be learned, or which cannot be learned except through the servile imitation of an individual, is not art.[4] In keeping with this understanding, art is not identified with the artist, but is superior to him. I only become an artist (and one can only become an artist, and not be one from the start) by receiving the art from other men who teach it to me, and, supposing that I enlarge this art with an invention, it would be artistic only if it could be taught to others, and thus only if it is not my own exclusive good, that is, only if it is not tied to qualities that are unique to my person, such as an inimitable flourish. If art is a knowledge that I put to work, it always surpasses me: it cannot go wrong, but I can, by departing from its rules or by applying them incorrectly. Grammar does not contain mistakes, but the grammarian can commit them.

That art is the making of a work means that everything in it must be considered in the *clarity of the work*. Art as human operation fades away within this clarity, which orients art from its origin. All is ordered to this clarity, and art is not concerned with anything that does not concern the work itself. The intentions of the artist are not important, nor are his interior perfections or imperfections. It is in a Greek manner that Saint Thomas Aquinas, who could never be suspected of immoralism or of estheticism, brushes aside as impertinent any consideration of art that turns aside from the making of a work and the work done. "For a craftsman as such is commendable, not for the intention with which he does a work, but for the quality of the work."[5] For, he adds later, "it is not in the artist that one finds the good of an art, but rather in the thing itself that he produces." All production is transitive: it is completed elsewhere than within us, in a thing henceforth independent of us; and when we consider *making,* its perfection, if it has any, "is not a perfection of the maker, but of the thing made" (*non est perfectio facientis, sed facti*).[6] At issue is not whether the artist forgets himself in the work or for its benefit, for there are ways of forgetting oneself that are still too preoccupied with the self, ways to efface oneself where one shows oneself drawing aside, through a sort of narcissistic preterition. He who makes a work does not even have to forget himself, so much does what he has to do occupy him, and forget for him everything that is not a part of this making. Saint Thomas says that "art does not require of the artist that he act well, but that his work be good. Rather would it be necessary for the thing made to act well, for example that a knife should cut well."[7] Let us leave to this exemplary knife its sharp edge: it cuts at the root of every cult of the artist, who was never, either in Antiquity or the Middle Ages, distinguished from the craftsman, the same word, in Greek and in Latin, referring to them both. Why? Artists and craftsmen are, in the etymological sense of the terms, workers; they do works, they work: to think about art and to think about the doing of work are rigorously identical. In the sixteenth century, Guillaume du Bartas, on the second page of his *Semaine ou création du monde*, could, without seeing any harm in it, speak of God as the "Worker of workers, all powerful and all knowing." When the craftsman and the artist were separated, the unity of the human making of works was broken.

Late Greek thought institutes another economy between art, the artist, and the work, one that breaks with the primacy of the work and no longer sees the highest clarity within it. But the case remains that human art, as production, is still not a creation. Thus Plotinus, in a famous page from his treatise on intellectual beauty, still considers that the artist is inferior to the art itself, but also (and this is new) states that the work made by the artist, far from being the end of art, has only an inferior beauty in comparison to the beauty of art, meaning, to the ideas and to the harmonies of the intellectual world that the artist contemplates. The beauty that the sculptor has introduced into the formless stone was first within him. But it was so "not by his equipment of eyes and hands but by his participation in his art."[8] The Platonic term "participation" clearly indicates that art is above the artist, in the intellectual realm: it must not be confused with the thoughts of the artist himself, or with his projects. The intellectual music that precedes sensible music is the work of no musician,[9] and alone makes the musician what he is. "The beauty, therefore, exists in a far higher state in the art; for it has not come over into the stone, but remains [in itself], and it is another beauty, derivative and minor, [that comes into the stone]."[10] Plotinus here applies to beauty his theory of the two acts, according to which, for example, the heat that is in the fire itself and that which radiates around it are not the same heat: that which derives from an act is another act, inferior to its origin. The beauty that belongs to art is "greater and more beautiful" than that which is inscribed in the exteriority of the work produced by this art. "It is necessary," writes Plotinus, "that everything which produces originarily is in itself more powerful than that which is produced." The context shows that this is not about the artist, but about art, or, in other terms, that it concerns the intelligible at the origin of the sensible. The clarity from the work has been diminished and weakened if art is always more beautiful than the particular works of art; nevertheless, despite all of this, the artist has not become a creator. And the metaphysics of Plotinus would forbid posing any sort of analog to an art for the first principal from which everything issues, even though he will, on a lesser plane, affirm that "the activity peculiar to life is artistic," as had the Stoics.[11]

On the path of "divine art," a new question appears. When some Christian thinkers will make an artist of God the creator—indeed, the supreme artist—this will have as a consequence a radical overturning of the relations that ancient philosophy had established between nature and art. Instead of being first, nature will become secondary with regard to art, the world being in its entirety a work of divine art. Even the natural will become artificial in its essence. Did this thinking of an originary art, at the foundation of nature itself, appear with Christianity, or did it have precedents in ancient philosophy? There exist at least two precedents, very different from one another, but each of great importance. The first is an astonishing and singular page from Book Ten of Plato's *Laws*, where, in criticizing theses that, in an impious manner to his mind, make everything arise from nature and chance, and thus deny the existence of the gods and reduce the importance and

the efficacy of art to insignificance, Plato comes to reverse
the traditional situation of nature and of art, of *phusis* and
of *tekhnè*. The primacy of the soul as organizer of the world
over all that is corporal will bring about a primacy of
tekhnè, of art over nature, or at least (and the difference is
simply one of scale) of art over that which the authors that
Plato has undertaken to refute call nature and the natural.

> The soul being counted among the primary things, it must
> be that what is most important and primordial among
> works and activities comes from art, while that which is
> from nature, and nature herself—to use the mistaken termi-
> nology of our opponents—is posterior and must result, as a
> subordinate thing, from art and from intelligence.[12]

But the remainder of the passage shows that, if the word
nature is taken according to its true meaning, then the soul,
being more original than the body, is also quite natural,
and is even preeminently so. The primacy of art over
nature becomes in fact the primacy of the proper and true
meaning of nature over a derived and improper meaning.[13]
And the art attributed to the soul is not a creative art.

The second testimony from ancient thought in favor of an
originary art is that of Stoicism, in the person of Zeno of
Cittium. Cicero expounds it, and we must note that the verb
"to create" figures in the definition of art. It is worth remembering that, in Stoic physics, fire plays the decisive role.

> Now Zeno gives this definition of nature: "nature (he says)
> is an artist fire (*ignem artificiosum*), proceeding methodically
> to the work of generation." For he holds that the special
> function of an art is to create (*creare*) and generate, and that
> what in the processes of our arts is done by the hand is done
> with far more skilful artistry by nature, that is, as I said, by
> that artist fire which is the master of the other arts. And on
> this theory, while each department of nature is artistic, in
> the sense of having a method or path marked out for it to
> follow, the nature of the work itself, which encloses and con-
> tains all things in its embrace, is styled by Zeno not merely
> artist-like but is actually an artist, whose foresight plans out
> the work to serve its use and purpose in every detail.[14]

The "eminent beauty" of the world thus presents a singularity for the Stoics: it is the beauty of a work of divine art that contains *in itself* the art through which it is so beautiful. Master of all the arts, the artist fire, the pure *lekhnikon*, is at once both the supreme art and the supreme artist: it is immanent in its work, it dwells within it. There is no need to fear that a work in which the artist dwells might ever decline in beauty. The artist maintains it from the inside, so that it is never left to itself. The economy here of relations between art, artist, and work is completely new. As for nature, active and formative nature, it is, contrary to the earlier Greek philosophy, defined by art itself. The most intimate part of nature is at the same time the fullness of art. What characterizes this art is its ease, and its virtuosity, which makes light of resistance and obstacles. Seen against such an artistic nature, how laborious, difficult, and arduous all human art appears! A fault inside art, and something like an alienation of human art, shows itself here, doubtless for the first time with such sharpness. The very concept of art stems from, and can only stem from, a description and an analysis of human production, insofar as it is radically distinguished from natural transformations. With Stoicism, it is transferred to nature itself, in such a way that our art henceforward becomes an inferior art, an art that is much less artistic than the art of fire. Our art is no longer compared with whatever is other than art, but rather to another art, one that is infinitely more skilful and more powerful. This "artist fire" is divine, and Tertullian will say that Zeno defined God as "the craftsman (*factitatorem*) who has formed and ordered all."[15] But, for the Stoics, the divine itself is corporal, and if the word creation is employed by Cicero, it is assuredly not meant in the sense of a creation from nothing, but in the sense of a forming. Fire is precisely that which remains even when everything else is consumed by it. This art has nothing creative about it, in the biblical sense, nor does it lead to thinking of the human artist as a creator. We are still within a way of thinking about production and transformation, despite the upheavals affecting the concept of art. The divinity has indeed become an artist, but this divinity is not the creator God.

When, with Christian thought, the idea of creation in the strong sense is finally made free,[16] it is that which separates God from every human artist that becomes emphasized. Nevertheless, comparisons between the world and a work of art appear here and there, above all as an aid to the pondering of the world's beauty. The truly decisive moment in this regard presents itself in the philosophy of Saint Augustine: it comprises not merely a fleeting or circumstantial analogy, but a veritable doctrine of the *ars divina*, the divine art, which will ever after be a perpetual source of inspiration for other thinkers. In one of the expositions he undertakes, this divine art is immediately put into relation with human art, at the same time that their difference is underscored: "That supreme art of the omnipotent God through which all things have been made from nothing, which is also called his Wisdom, also works through artists to produce things of beauty and proportion, although they do not produce from nothing, but from a given material. . . ."[17] Saint Augustine is thinking here of sculptors. God's creative art is prolonged in human art, which itself is no longer creative. How? What the artist impresses bodily onto a body—the work's proportions and harmony—he receives in his mind from the supreme wisdom, which moreover conferred such proportions and harmony to the universe "with yet even more art" (*longe artificiosius*). The divine art at work in nature has "more power and excellence by far" than that which human artists give proof of in their statues. The human artist must not forget the "supreme wisdom" from which he draws his powers. Indeed, he stands in a double dependence, which shows itself in the ways in which he is not a creator. The first dependence is in relation to the world and its elements: able only to transform, and not to create, the artist needs a matter to work upon. The second dependence is in relation to the norms and models of his art, for he cannot invent them himself with his mind alone, but can only receive them from the divine wisdom, or the divine art.

Nevertheless, if human art, despite these differences, prolongs and imitates divine art according to its own fashion, it possesses by this very fact an eminent dignity. Art itself becomes a relation with God. Consequently, the study of the procedures of human art can, for Saint Augustine, constitute a path toward the divine art that is at its foundation. This apologetics through appeal to the beauty of art as well as nature, thereby making a return to that which renders them possible, crops up often in Saint Augustine's philosophical works. The goal here is not to study it in all its aspects, but only to ponder the consequences for thinking about the work and about art that result from the introduction of an artist God. They appear clearly, in conclusion to this apologetics of beauty, in the treatises *De vera religione* and *De libero arbitrio*. The first affirms that neither things nor our senses can lead the soul astray: if the soul makes a mistake, it has only itself to blame. And Saint Augustine continues,

> It is sin which deceives souls, when they seek something that is true but abandon or neglect truth. They love the works of the artificer more than the artificer or his art, and are punished by falling into the error of expecting to find the artificer and his art in his works, and when they cannot do so they think that the works are both the art and the artificer. God is not offered to the corporeal senses, and transcends even the mind.[18]

With the *ars divina*, the work thus undergoes a profound change of status with relation to Greek thinking about the *ergon*. Certainly there is still a clarity in works, but this clarity refers back just short of itself, toward the source that emitted it. The work is no longer that upon which the gaze must stop, or that beside which it must stay: it must rouse and move the viewer toward its author. If the artist is none other than God, and his work the creature, it goes without saying that the artist is infinitely superior to his work. But is it the same for human art? Saint Augustine lays down an equivalence between the strictly religious proposition, incontestable in its order, according to which "those who not only love, but also serve the creature rather than the creator"[19] make themselves guilty of a serious infidelity and a heavy sin, and the proposition according to which we must consider as misguided he who prefers the work to the artist, or he who does not seek the artist through his work. The second surely does not present the evidence of the first, unless art is thought of completely otherwise than according to the clarity of works. To return to the example of Saint Thomas Aquinas, what do the intentions of the cutler matter to me? What matters is that the knife cut well. And what exactly would it mean that the cutler has expressed himself through his knife?

In the artistic analogy applied to divine creation there dawns a conception according to which the highest function of the work is to manifest and to express its author. The treatise *De libero arbitrio* states it sharply:

> O Wisdom, O Light most pleasing to a mind made pure! Woe to those who forsake your guidance and grope about among your shadowy imitations and, more enamored of your signs than of you, are forgetful of what you wish to intimate. For you never cease to intimate your nature and excellence to us, and the entire beauty of created things consists in these signs. The artist, too, through the beauty of his work, intimates in a way to the viewer that he should not fasten his attention there completely but should so scan the beauty of the artistic work that he will turn his thoughts back fondly upon he who made it. Those who love the things you make instead of yourself are like men who listen to the eloquence of a wise man. In their overeagerness to hear his beautiful voice and the skilful cadence of his words, they neglect the primary importance of his thoughts for which the spoken words were to serve as signs.[20]

The reach of these lines is considerable.

According to a theme destined for a rich future up through Berkeley and German Romanticism, the works of God, his creatures, here become a language by which God addresses himself to us and speaks to us. The final comparison underscores that divine art is a language. And the peril into which this language throws us is to attach us to what signifies rather than to what is signified, thus making what is signified become insignificant at the same time that we ourselves become idolaters. But, if the signifier is the creatures' form and the signified the divine thought, then these works of divine art have their meaning outside and above themselves. In a spare, strong formulation, Henri Focillon, after having insisted on the temptation to confuse the form with the image and above all with the sign, says: "The sign signifies, while the form signifies itself."[21] In this sense, Saint Augustine here reduces the forms to signs, to signs of God. This is the first decision made in this important page. The second is to lay down as the highest meaning of the work the manifestation of its author. We must not, according to this conception, remain close to the beauty of the work: the verbal play between *percurrat oculis* and *recurrat adfectu,* between looking at the work and clinging to the artist, is quite clear.

Now, the world is not a work among others, but properly speaking the Great Work, and creation is distinguished from all production: one therefore might imagine that, in a comparison between human and divine art, the accent would be placed even more on their dissemblance than on their resemblance. To think of the created world as manifestation of the Absolute is not the same as thinking of every work of art as destined, before all else, to express its author. It is thus remarkable that Saint Augustine considers it self-evident that, in *human* art, it is necessary to love the author more than the work. The consequences of such a decision are without measure: the power to make a work is more than the work, the clarity of the work is not inaugural, but only reflected and lunar; it comes from elsewhere and leads us elsewhere, toward the mind of the artist. The spirit of art is thus not to be grasped first of all in the thing in which it is incarnated; it dwells beyond the life and presence of the artist himself, it signals to us across things that are only so many stages on the way to it.

How exactly does Saint Augustine think through this "divine art," which he identifies with the wisdom of God? It is the Son, the Word, the second person of the Trinity who forms the wisdom and the art by which God creates the world. He is the "one perfect Word to which nothing is lacking, which is like the art of the almighty and wise God *(ars quaedam omnipotentis atque sapientis Dei)*, full of all the unchanging principles of living beings."[22] If the divine art is a divine person, there is necessarily a total and perfect identity between the *art* and the *artist*, which are radically inseparable. The artist is nothing other than the living art, and the art is nothing other than the intimate life of the eternal artist. God has no need to work to be an artist. Here there is another revolution in the relations between the work, art, and the artist. It throws a new light upon the preceding analyses: indeed, if art and the artist are one, the work's reference back to the artist is alike to its reference back to the art itself that precedes it. The beauty of the work is a sign, certainly, but a sign of the complete form that founds it, and which not only has more beauty, but is beauty itself, perfect beauty. If the divine art, the artist Word, contains in himself the models of all things, according to which all things were made, then *the things are more beautiful in art than in themselves.* The beauty of art is the highest of all the beauties.

Saint Augustine affirms this expressly time and again: the knowledge the creature has "of itself" is, "so to speak, shadowy" by comparison with the knowledge that would be gained "in the art by which it was made."[23] Even the spirit, which pleases us more than corporeal light, "we do not value . . . in itself but in this art by which it was made."[24] The divine art, which is the Word, possesses in himself the being and the life of all that which is created. In him, in their source, things are eternally safe, from the beginning and forever sheltered from any alteration. Everything is said in the Word before being expressed or uttered outside. In art being is this immemorial promise that always already sustains us. "A worker," says Saint Augustine,

> makes a chest. First he has the chest in his art; for if he had it not in his art, from whence would he draw it out when he makes it? But the chest is not in art in the same manner as the chest which appears to the eyes. It exists invisibly in art, and it will be visible in the work. Behold, now it is made in the work: has it ceased to exist in art? No, the one is made in the work, and the other remains which exists in art; for that chest may rot, and another be fashioned according to that which exists in art. Pay attention, then, to the chest in art, and the chest as work (*arcam in arte, et arcam in opere*). The chest as work is not life, the chest in art is life, because the soul of the artist, where all these things are before they are produced outside, is living.[25]

Saint Augustine thus starts with human art before transferring the analysis to divine art. The new and decisive thesis from this page bears on the double presence of the chest: the chest such as it is found as model within the artist possesses not the properties of the physical chest, which will be of wood, have extension, and be perishable, but the properties of the soul of the artist. It lives from his life, and thus eludes decline. A spiritual chest thus precedes the material chest. And Saint Augustine can thus continue:

> Because the Wisdom of God, through which all things were made, contains everything according to art before it is made, therefore those things which are made through this art itself are not immediately life, but whatever has been made is life in this art. You see the earth, there is also an earth in art; you see the sky, there is also a sky in art; you see the sun and the moon, these, too, exist in art: but externally they are bodies, and in art they are life.

Divine art, and the being of things in it, take the place of the intelligible world of the Platonists, of which Plato himself never spoke. Everything there is living, inalterable, invisible, eternal, pure. But isn't every work then a decline and a sort of failure in relation to the very art that produces it? The art descends toward its works, condescends to its works, instead of raising itself toward them as toward its true and proper light. Even an idle art would still possess in itself this life that is higher than the life that can communicate itself to produced things. Such a fault line has something about it that seems irreparable.

In our century, the poetic word will assign for itself, according to an inverse symmetry, a mission analogous to that of the divine Word for Saint Augustine. If the latter gathers in from all eternity the being of things before they come to an existence doomed to decline, the word of the poet according to Rilke will gather in after the event the declining things to transfigure them, render them invisible, and save them by transforming them in ourselves, by offering them our own life. This is affirmed powerfully by the end of the *Ninth Duino Elegy:*

> Earth, isn't this what you want: an invisible
> re-arising in us? Is it not your dream
> to be one day invisible? Earth! invisible![26]

There is an earth in art, too. A famous letter to Witold von Hulewicz makes it explicit. As for Paul Claudel, while assuredly he does not replace the divine Word with the poetic word, but rather hinges the latter on the former, he too evokes an existence in art that escapes the decay of exterior existence:

> The leaf yellows and the fruit falls, but the leaf in my
>   verse does not perish,
> Nor the fruit either, nor the rose among roses!
> It perishes, but its name in the spirit that is my spirit
>   perishes no more.
> Here it is, escaping from time.[27]

It is enough to put these words opposite the following from Saint Augustine:

> The house which an architect builds was first in his art, and there, it was a better house, without age, without [possible] decay; however, to show forth this art, he makes a house, and so, in a manner, this house comes forth from the [first] house; and if the house should fall, the art remains (*ars manet*). So were all things that have been made in the Word of God.[28]

That the being in art and the being in the work come in a certain sense to oppose one another, because one refers back to divine thought and to ideas, and the other to the creature, shows the revolution introduced through these terms. The work perishes, art remains. Art is by its essence more beautiful than the work. The knowledge of art is clearer, the knowledge of works more obscure; the former is a daylight knowledge, the latter a twilight knowledge.[29]

At the dawn of Romanticism, Joseph Joubert, in his *Notebooks*, will sketch a metaphysics of beauty that is paradoxical in that, on the one hand, it takes up, doubtless by diverse mediations more than by a direct knowledge, fundamental Augustinian theses, and on the other hand refers to the being of beauty in a way that is radically opposed to the ancient way of thinking, in solidarity with which Saint Augustine remains. When Joubert writes: "All that is beautiful is indeterminate,"[30] when he sets out his aesthetic of resounding sounds, of the spacious, of the vague and the veiled, he is, as with his fragmentary and unfinished writing, properly romantic. But beauty is for him ideal and takes its source in God himself, even though Joubert does not speak expressly of divine art. "That which is truly beautiful is that which resembles its idea. Thus we say every day of a man with good health, or of a woman with a fine freshness, She is freshness or He is good health personified."[31] If, as he affirms, "there is no beauty but the idea," the beauty of art surpasses natural beauty, for "a work of art must have the appearance not of a reality, but of an idea," and "our ideas . . . are always more noble, and more beautiful, and better at touching the soul than the objects that they represent."[32] Such a beauty still refers back to God, because "God is the source of the beautiful."[33]

According to Joubert not only must one climb back up from the work to the artist, but the latter is again like the sun of its works, a third sun, between the natural sun and the sun of spirits, God himself. The following fragment shows clearly the subordinate character of the work, which does not show itself by itself:

> "See everything in God" to find everything beautiful. For, in order to find beautiful objects beautiful, it is necessary that the sun be behind and the light be all around. And in order to find the works of men beautiful, it is necessary that the soul of those who made them be behind, so to speak, and that the soul show itself all around and that we see the works contained there. That is the sun and the light that must illuminate objects.[34]

The spiritual presence of the artist is that without which the work cannot become truly manifest. The work is no longer the Greek *ergon*, whose dignity lies precisely in its detaching itself from its author, being truly in the world, standing in its own clarity.

Thus for Joubert God is an artist, or comparable to an artist,[35] even if Joubert refuses to name man a creator.[36] But, when he sees in art an "imitation of the divine," it is in a way that is totally unique to him: "Transparency, the diaphanous, the scrap of matter, the magical; the imitation of the divine who made all things out of little and, so to speak, out of nothing: this is one of the essential characteristics of poetry."[37] The point of comparison between the human artist and God thus lies not in supreme creative power, but in economy and restraint. It is in sobriety that we resemble God. A poet imitates God when he refuses himself streams of eloquence and the invasion of space by the sonority of his voice, and instead allows a few words to illuminate the silence, making much with the least of possible means. Little material for much space,[38] such is the demanding law of divine creation and of human art, according to Joubert: he is a thinker of spatiality and of the distant echoing of the tiny.

Joubert does not go to the endpoint of the movement that divinizes the artist as "creator," but his recovery of Augustinian theses is significant in that it inverts their perspective. For Saint Augustine, the analogy of art is a way to think better about the preexistence of ideas in the divine Word and the process of creation: it goes from human art to divine art as if from the known to the unknown. For Joubert, in the opposite way, the divine creation is a model for thinking about what human art is and what it must be: man is thought of after God, human art by way of divine art. It would be naïve to think that this is a theocentric movement: on the contrary, to take God as the point of departure to ponder art is, even if the word is not uttered, to consider man as creator, and to tend to efface the dissemblance between his art and divine art. Theological schemas haunt the analysis of human production, but, in so doing, decenter themselves and lose their site and their original meaning.

After these evocations of modernity, it is fitting to come back to the history of divine art. Augustinian thought of God the artist is prolonged and developed throughout the Middle Ages. John Scottus Eriugena in the ninth century and Saint Bonaventure in the thirteenth form two decisive moments of this tradition. The first introduces into the heart of the divine life itself the distinction between art and the artist. "The artist is the cause of his art," he writes, "while art is not the cause of its artist, but art itself precedes all the things that subsist in it, by it, and from it, for it is the cause."[39] If, in the Trinity, the Son is the Father's art, through which the world is created, the Father, for his part, is properly speaking the *artifex*, the artist, engendering and preceding his art. The generation of art by the artist is the eternal condition of possibility for the production of things by art. The "all-powerful artist" is not only God, but God the Father. God is at the same time the art and the artist, but under two distinct relations. The introduction of artistic concepts into the Trinitarian life has something intellectually thrilling and surprising about it: the artistic analogy serves no longer only to think of the relation of the world as work to God the creator, but to think of the relations internal to God himself. The first act of the supreme artist is not a *work*, but his art, which is his Son. The work's share diminishes in certain respects, at the same time that the art becomes properly a universal model, since it includes the Absolute itself. Moreover, that the entire creation is thought of by Eriugena as a theophany, a manifestation of God, prepares a way of thinking about expression and does even more to ensure the artistic analogy.[40]

Just as important is the fact that Eriugena, pondering man as the image of God, lends him a creative power, and employs in connection with this the words "to create" at numerous times, even if this is not in the same sense as for God. An image of the relation between the Father as artist and the Son as art exists in the human soul between the intellect and reason. Reason is an art. And it is the place where the intellect, "by an admirable operation of its science, creates by means of knowledge (*creat per cognitionem*)" all that it has received from God.[41] Further on, Eriugena affirms that the human soul, "made by God in the image of God out of nothing, . . . creates its own body (*corpus sum creat*), though this is not out of nothing, but out of something." The soul "creates for itself a body in which it can openly manifest its hidden actions, which are by themselves invisible."[42] We are thus the creator artists of our bodies, and, just as God exerts his providence on the entire creation, we exert our own providence on the totality of the body that we have formed.[43] The human artist is still an imitator, but it is no longer nature that he imitates, as for the Greeks, but the supreme artist, the artist God.[44] Art imitates art, a higher art from which it is derived, and which continues to act through it, as Saint Augustine had already affirmed.

It begins to appear that the movement by which the human artist will come to take himself for a creator does not issue from a profane tradition wherein rebellious man takes the place of the God he rejects. Quite to the contrary, it is born in Christian theology itself, and more precisely in the Augustinian lineage, where Christianity and Platonic philosophy meet. This lineage is the place of a radical and profound thinking of humility, which holds not the least paradox in regard to what it will wind up engendering in spite of its intentions. The Renaissance authors by whom man will be most forcefully thought of as creator will belong to this tradition: the continuity is clear up to Marsilio Ficino and Nicholas of Cusa. It is they who carried this movement to its term, the point of departure in turn for a new history. In the Middle Ages, between the time of Eriugena and that of Saint Bonaventure, Saint Anselm insists instead on the dissemblance between the artist's operation and that of the creator God, a dissemblance that is more vivid than any resemblance.[45] Saint Bonaventure, for his part, meditates with unequalled power upon the divine art that is the Word, and stands as the great thinker of the world as expression of God.

Approached in such ways, the theology of the Word as *ars divina* presents two unbalancing aporias that threaten to render vain its thinking. The first lies in the infinite superiority of the artist over the work. If God envisaged as artist is always beyond and above his work, and if this work, far from exhausting his power, merely proposes, whatever its intrinsic beauty, a sample that could always be imagined to be more perfect without ever equaling the integral perfection of its author, is there not, in addition to an insurmountable fault between the artist and the work, a space of indetermination? God would thus only speak of himself in his work in hints, and in an almost ironical fashion. He would be a lesser artist than man who could throw himself completely into his work, giving himself to it entirely in its highest incandescence. The second aporia lies in the superiority of art and of the being that is in the divine art, over the finished work and over the being that is in the finished work. If things are more beautiful in God than in themselves, if their immemorial, archetypal past, their being at the source has a splendor that cannot be equaled by the splendor that they have in existing or in standing outside of God, why were they deployed and created? As the praise of divine art sharpens, does it not become the affirmation of the superfluity and the imperfection of its work? These difficulties have a common center, and their resolution will follow the same path. Malebranche's philosophy testifies to these difficulties not being the least bit imaginary: pondering the incommensurability of the divine infinity and the world's finitude, he will come to speak of the "low and humiliating position of the Creator," and, against the tradition, to see, at first, the act by which God creates a world outside of himself, though all-powerful, as an abasement of God.[46] What sense is there in making a work if the work never matches up to the level of the art?

The incarnation of the Word, and the possibilities that it opens for man, resolve these difficulties. The union of God and man in a single person is the union of divine art and one of its works in a single being. Nothing can be more perfect, and the principle of indetermination introduced by the superiority of the artist over the work here finds its limit and ceases to play a role. God can make a masterpiece by uniting himself to his work. Saint Bonaventure shows this powerfully with yet another artistic analogy. The medieval theme of two books is well known: it distinguishes and unites two expressions of God, the world and the Bible, the book of the world and the book of Scripture, each one referring us to their author, and each one able to enlighten the other. But, for Saint Bonaventure, this theme is enlarged and deepened by another book, the *liber intus scriptus*, the book written on the inside, separated from the world as *liber foris scriptus*, the book written on the outside.

This inner book is the divine art itself, divine wisdom, the Word insofar as it contains the archetypes of all that can be created. When God incarnates himself and the Word assumes the humanity of Jesus, the inner book of divine art and the outer book of the creature unite. Jesus Christ is both at the same time, the art and the work together.[47] And it is significant that Saint Bonaventure sometimes speaks of these two books with regard to man in order to oppose him to the angel, who is the reader and contemplator of the inner book, and to the animals other than man, which are devoted solely to the outer book of the world. Man, in whom the two books meet without merging, can become the place where the beauty of things outside of the divine art refers and leads back to their beauty in the divine art itself, the place where things, without being cancelled out, sing of their origin, with all that their voices possess in their own right. The second aporia is thus resolved. And yet this does not confer upon man a role as creator. To sing the song of the real world is a higher and more dignified task than the creation of fictional worlds.

The thought of the Renaissance brings its own inflections to this long history of the *ars divina* and its imitation by man. Without being effaced completely, the distance between the two arts is reduced. Profound differences of accent and meaning result, depending on whether the divine art is thought of above all with the distance of the artist from the work as its end and fulfillment (creation), or whether, instead, the union of the artist with the work is seen as its end and fulfillment, thereby elevating the work above itself (incarnation). That is, profound differences result when divine art is thought of according to natural theology or according to revealed theology. Marsilio Ficino, in his *Theologia platonica*, the very title of which indicates the former perspective, multiplies the arguments that might signal the grandeur of the soul and its proximity to the divine. Among these, art figures importantly. Ficino nevertheless seems to make the task difficult for himself from the outset by generalizing the notion of art. Thus he speaks of art being exercised in natural processes and in animal functions.[48] God inserts his art into every natural thing. The various arts are distributed among the animals, but each species exercises only one. If there is art everywhere, its possession no longer seems to be a human privilege. But right away this difference presents itself: all the arts "are gathered together in the unique rational human species, even while distributed among each individual." In this, the individual who specializes in an act does not cease to have a relation to the totality of the arts. And human art distinguishes itself from animal art for Ficino in that we "receive" the arts (that is to say "the kinds of things and the rules of the arts") from "God without any intermediary," in that "each receives them all," even if he does not cultivate them all, and, finally, in that we exercise them "by the free judgment of reason," and not "by the impelling force of nature." These kinds of things and these rules "are in us in a perfect and clear manner," almost as they are in God and in the angels, even in the form of images.[49] This richness of human art leads Ficino to higher and higher praises.

To begin with, we are, thanks to art, nature's rivals: "What a marvelous thing! The human arts by themselves make all that nature herself makes, as if we were not the slaves of nature, but rather her emulators." Ficino then cites, pell-mell, trompe-l'œil painting and automata, among which he describes a scale mode of the sky. "In a work, man imitates all the works of divine nature, and perfects, corrects, and ameliorates the works of inferior nature."[50] This rivalry with nature will little by little become a rivalry with God himself. "The power of man is almost alike to the divine nature because, by himself, that is to say by his reflection and by his art, man governs himself."[51] Here we find an old theme from the theology of man in the image of God, with man's mastery over the universe and over living beings making him a sort of god on earth, a second providence for the other creatures as much as for himself. Ficino develops two aspects successively. Dominating all the living and, in one way or another, ranging across all the elements, through his intelligence or by his works, man "fills the role of God, because he dwells in all the elements and because, present on the earth, he is yet not absent from the ether." Man is equally divine by his providence: "Universal providence is proper to God, who is the universal cause; consequently man, who provides (*providet*) in a general manner for all beings, living and not living, is in a certain measure a god (*est quidam Deus*)."[52] He is "the God of the animals," the "God of the elements," the "God of all materials, he who works, transforms, and fashions them all." Even if the word creator is not uttered with regard to man, the divine nature of human art, which imitates the "artist God of nature (*Deum naturae artificem*)," is the equivalent. In art, man is like God.

Above all, according to Ficino, comprehension of the making of a work of art makes us equal to its author: he who "can discover why or how a work, constructed with art by a skilful craftsman, was realized" possesses the "same artistic talent (*ingenio artis*)."[53] Supposing I have the same means at my disposal, I can make something if I understand how it is made. Knowledge becomes operative. Ficino draws the inescapable consequence, and it is of capital importance that he formulates it with regard to the heavens—and thus with regard to that which escapes all possible productive art:

> Because man has seen the order of the movement of the heavens, its progression and its proportions or its results, how could one deny that he possesses almost the same genius, so to speak, as the author of the heavens, and that he could, to a certain degree, make the heavens (*caelos facere*), if he found instruments and celestial matter, since he makes them now, certainly, out of another matter, yet completely similar in their arrangement?[54]

Whoever can make a planetarium could make planets! This phrase, with its incomparable and powerfully innovating seriousness, and which would have appeared to the Ancients and the medievals as truly mad, presents itself as evidential. Assuredly, there is a circle here, which causes the very idea of creation to evaporate: after the human schema of artistic production has been applied to divine creation, and the knowledge of manufacture has become identical to a know-how, we are assimilated to the state of virtual creators, to whom only the means are lacking. But creation took place precisely without means, without instruments or matter. After having assimilated creation to a calculus, Leibniz also could affirm that our intelligence differs from God's in degree, and not in nature.[55] The artistic analogy turns against its initial intention, which was to underscore the incomparable grandeur of God.

It is decisive that the first site where man comes to think of himself as creator belongs not to art in the modern sense of beaux-arts, but to art in the ancient sense, where it is first of all knowledge *(savoir)*. For Ficino, to understand, by astronomy, the functioning of the heavens, or the work of God, and thus to understand their 'facture' (a word that Novalis will oppose to nature), is by right, if not in reality, to be capable of making them. Know-how, which is the ancient *tekhnè*, could, according to this conception, by right be applied to every thing, because every thing is the product of a divine art. Art by definition had as its domain the contingent; the necessary, whose realm was the heavens, escaped it. With Ficino, human art opens for itself a horizon wherein even the model of that which cannot be mastered has now become a part of it. Already at issue here is technology in the modern sense, if all can by right become an object of production. The heavens are no longer unmakeable, nor makeable only by divine art. Their contemplation is no longer the peaceful joy of a gaze brought to bear upon that which cannot be otherwise: it is only the preface to an operative knowledge, opening onto a virtual production.

The astonishing fourteenth book of the *Theologia platonica* establishes that "all the effort *(conatus)* of our soul is to become god." Enumerating twelve divine attributes, Ficino describes all human existence in its diverse forms and possibilities as a perpetual tension toward them. "Everywhere men refer all their acts to the possession of these attributes, and they aim at and reach toward nothing other than their complete possession."[56] Far from being an opportunity to underscore human pride and folly, this theme serves Ficino as a multiform proof of the greatness and the immortality of our soul, the masterpiece of God the creator. The disproportion of human desire is not a sign of aberration, but instead shows that God alone can satisfy us. This gives Ficino, in his description of human *anxietas,* a tone that seems to foretell Pascal.[57] Among the divine attributes, Ficino mentions that of being "the author of all things" and that of being "above everything." "These too," he adds, "are coveted by our soul." Art is the preeminent scene of the desire to be like the creator. "By the different arts it [the soul] vies with all the works of God, and thus accomplishes everything, like God (*ita instar Dei efficit omnia*)."[58] And as for the fact that man "will not suffer something to be shielded from his domination": it is proof of his greatness, and of his quest for the divine.

Art is thus twice over the site of a divinization of man: first of all, by the exercise of his arts and the production of his works, man becomes like God; the radical difference between human production and divine creation does not serve as an opportunity for meditation upon finitude. Second, man's comprehension of the divine art at work in the world elevates him above this very work, and makes his relationship with God that of one artist to another, each knowing, even to different degrees, the secrets of art. This becomes more a relation of connivance than of praise. The soul, writes Ficino, "is so close to God that, insinuating itself into the secrets of divine intelligence, it knows God's work, which is to say the order of the universe. The intelligence of the order of the universe is superior to this order itself, because this order was established and is governed by the intelligence."[59] Certainly, it might seem later on that Ficino tempers this praise of art by showing that, to a certain degree, it is something we hold in common with the beasts, while that which man possesses in his own right, and is alone in possessing, is "religion."[60] But such is not the case, for this has to do with another problem, and the difference between, on the one hand, human art, which vies with God, and the ability of animals, on the other, remains expressly emphasized.

With Ficino, we come to the endpoint of this history that first made God an artist, then divinized the human artist. It is clear at present that it is through and through a theological history and not part of a revolt against or an uprooting from theology. We need to measure the paradoxes: for Aristotle, if art formed a preeminent site of human greatness and superiority, it could have nothing to do with the divine, and was not a site for divinization. To compare God to an artist, even with all the possible correctives, would have appeared to him absurd and unworthy of God. The knowing that brings us close to God is thus in no way a know-how. Know-how is that which permits man as such to transform his weakness into force and his indigence into resource. Art thus can only become a site for divinization if God first enters into art, and becomes an artist. He is not one originally in Revelation, but becomes one in a history where Christian Platonism dominates. From the moment that the artistic analogy unfolds in thinking about the creative act and the relation of God to the world, a decision is taken with unbounded consequences, stronger than any intention, and above all stronger than any good intention. Little by little, the dissimilar character of this analogy fades, indeed is doomed to fade, at the same time as its christological keystone, which recalls this dissimilarity. Ways of thinking originally tied to Christianity, even though the tie is not a necessary one, are carried away by their own weight, which dissociates them from Christianity. They are at the source of modern thinking about art in its fundamental concepts. The Renaissance, in this respect, is certainly not a renaissance of ancient thought, for ancient thought never regarded production as creation.

Just as much as that of Ficino, the lively thought of Nicholas of Cusa expressly accomplishes the transformation of man into creator, the image of the divine art. It takes up and develops Augustinian themes in its own characteristic way. The world is an "artifice," a work of divine art (*mundi artificium*), and Nicholas of Cusa, after having exposed the human analogy of the creation of syllogistic art by the master and the mortal inventor, transposes the schema to the divine creation of the world.[61] An entire chapter of *De docta ignorantia* bears on "the admirable divine art in the creation of the world and of the elements." Visible things, their grandeur, their beauty, and their order lead us to wonder in front of the divine art that made them spring up into being. In the creation of the world, God made use of arithmetic, geometry, music, and astronomy: "of these arts we too make use" in our investigations of the world. For Nicholas of Cusa as for Saint Augustine, we know ourselves better in God than we do in ourselves. "If you want to know something about us, seek it in our Cause and Reason, not in us. There you will find all things, while seeking one thing. And only in Him will you be able to discover yourself."[62]

But what interests Nicholas of Cusa in this order is the living relation of our arts to the divine art, and not only the contemplation of the works of this divine art. "All the human arts are images of the infinite and divine art," he writes, before adding: "All finite art thus comes from the infinite art. And thus it will be necessary that the infinite art be the model for all the arts, the principle, the medium, the end, the rule, the measure, the precision, and the perfection."[63] In "the absolute creative art, subsisting by itself," the art and the artist, the magisterium and the master, coincide with each other. This seems to separate radically the divine art from our own. But "our mind is a certain force

that possesses an image of the divine art. From there follows that all things which dwell in the absolute art dwell
truly in our mind, in the mode of images. Our mind is created by the creative art, as if this art wanted to create itself":
since God cannot create a God, he creates his image, and
thus Nicholas of Cusa makes a comparison with the self-
portrait of a painter. Between two images, the most perfect
is not necessarily, he shows, the best likeness. An image that
is more of a likeness, and yet is dead is less perfect than an
image that is less of a likeness but more alive, and which
has in itself the power to turn itself toward its model, and to
render itself there more conformed. Thus it is that our
mind—considered, again in Augustinian fashion, as the
image of God the Trinity—is in its way "a perfect and living
image of infinite art."[64] An image of art is itself an artist
image: it is living because it is an artist. The foundation is
laid for man to be, in art, a creator.

And Nicholas of Cusa indeed names him so:

> Consider that Hermes Trismegiste says that man is a second
> God. For, just as God is the creator of real beings and of nat-
> ural forms, so too man is the creator of artificial beings and
> forms. These are nothing other than likenesses of his intel-
> lect, just as God's creatures are likenesses of the divine intel-
> lect. This is how man possesses an intellect that is a likeness
> to the divine intellect in the creative act (*in creando*). From
> this it follows that he creates likenesses of the likenesses of
> the divine intellect, just as the artificial exterior figures are
> likenesses of the natural inner form. Thus he takes the meas-
> ure of his intellect according to the power of his works, and
> in this way he takes the measure of the divine intellect, just
> as one measures the truth by its image.[65]

Moreover, the preceding chapter takes in a favorable
sense the famous sentence of Protagoras, according to
which man is the measure of all things, giving it, it is true,
a new meaning.

This sparkling of God's infinite art in the finite art of
man never leads Nicholas of Cusa to confuse the two, but

it does give a rigorous grounding to the idea of human "creation." In another of his works, he takes the example, whose everyday quality is thoroughly Platonic, of the spoon and the pot:

> The spoon, outside of its idea in our mind, possesses no model (*exemplar*). In fact, even if the sculptor or the painter takes his models in things, which he makes every effort to figure, this is certainly not the case with me when I produce spoons from wood, and plates and pots from clay. In this I indeed do not imitate the figure of any natural thing. It is simply by human art that such forms of spoons, of plates or of pots are led to their completion. My art is thus much more perfect than that which imitates created figures, and in this it is more similar to infinite art.[66]

This praise for that which is artificial through and through and of human origin doubtless runs counter to the modern distinction between the artist and the craftsman or artisan, because the potter here draws nearer to God than does the greatest of painters, but it nevertheless constitutes one of the foundations of modernity. The human "creator" is without models, he depends on nothing, he himself creates in himself his own models. And thus creation is first and foremost interior and spiritual; it takes place initially in the mind of the artist. "Creation" precedes the work and renders it possible.

Thus it is not by rhetorical hyperbole but rather according to rigorous theological determinations that man has become for himself a creator and can name himself as such. From the moment that this title is conferred upon him, man does not relinquish it easily. There is a veritable inflation of "creations" and of "creators" throughout the course of modernity, and even beyond it. Even when Rimbaud, in his plan to be "stealer of fire," denies that poetry had until that point been creation, he does so by granting, and considering it granted and thus decided, that poetry can and must become creation: "Civil servants, writers: author, creator, poet—this man has never existed!"[67] The foregoing shows

where and by whom this decision was made. To follow all
the stages in the overcoming of the work by the artist, and
the disastrous victory of "creating" over the "making of a
work" *(faire œuvre)*, would be a long and tedious history,
because each of us already knows the result. The examples
of resistance to such a destiny shine forth high and clear,
but they do not interrupt its course; rather, they stand like
islands outside of it. The imbalances already present in the
foundational theological gestures of this transposition of
creation to human art have gathered an ever-augmented
strength. The primacy of the "creator" over all that he can
create, over every work that would merely be a sample of
his power, bears within it, inevitably, idleness *(le désœuvre-
ment)*. In taking himself for God, man becomes an idle god,
capricious and arbitrary. There is no nostalgia or lamenta-
tion that could possibly break with this disorientation,
because such feelings are always tied in with what grieves
them, this being also what makes them live.

It is better to be at work. Every human work is manual:
always and everywhere it is our hands that work, even
when they do not labor. Heidegger can say, profoundly,
that even thought is *Handwerk*, work of the hand.[68] The
hands think and thought handles: this is the very humanity of man. Divine creation takes place by the spoken word
alone, an incommunicable word that makes being spring
forth from nothing: put strictly, God, in creating, does not
make works, and we do not create when we make, with
our hands, a work, even if it is a work of words. It does not
lessen human art to recall it to its perpetual condition. All
human dignity is in our hands. The forgetting of the hand,
despite the apparent exaltation that accompanies it, is the
forgetting of man, and of the world with which our hands
have their dealings. Such is the danger of "creation."

Poets teach us to listen to language, and the faded word
main d'œuvre regains all of its resonance when Pierre
Reverdy gives it as the title to one of his most important
collections. The hand is present from first to last in this

book, in poems separated by many years. Everything begins with an early-rising hand:

> Il faut attendre l'or
> Atteindre le réveille-matin de la lumière
> Le courant incertain de l'air
> La main.

> It is necessary to wait for the gold
> To reach for the alarm clock of light
> The uncertain draft of air
> The hand.[69]

And in the song of twilight that forms the last poem of the collection, and ends with the word *silence*, we read several lines before the end: "The hands are without shelter."[70] The very titles of certain poems give meaning again to expressions that we no longer hear: *"Hommes de main hommes de peine,"*[71] *"Main-morte,"*[72] *"De la main à la main."*[73] Everything that is given and received goes from hand to hand *(de la main à la main)*, every gift is manual, every man is a strong-arm man *(homme de main)*. Isidore of Seville derived *manus* from *munus*, the gift, the present, the favor.[74] "It is the hand," he said, "that makes everything, and distributes everything; it is by the hand that we receive and that we give." It is not one of our organs, for we are only men through it and in it. The dignity of manual labor *(la main d'œuvre)*, of the hand at work, begs another name than that of creation to be recognized. Our hands know this much better than we do, and our works have more lucidity than we ourselves do. Opposing the idea that "the work is the artist's *product*," Claudel, in a letter, wrote:

> The idea that is becoming more and more clear to me is that, on the contrary, it is the work that is primary, that fulfils itself, often in spite of the author and the obstacles that he places in front of it, and that what we take for creative conditions is only insignificant decor, detritus, surmounted resistance, or simply a condition, a secondary cause, a momentary coloring and developer, a wake, a disheartening witness to the ignorance within good intention.[75]

NOTES

1. Isa. 29:16, cf. Jer. 18:6. Cf. Curtius, *European Literature*, Ex. 21.
2. Heb. 11:10. The Latin gives *artifex*.
3. Heidegger, *Aristotle's Metaphysics Theta, 1–3*, 117.
4. Aristotle, *Metaphysics*, Alpha, 1.
5. Thomas Aquinas, *Summa Theologiae*, Ia IIae, q. 57, a. 3; ed. Anton C. Pegis, *Basic Writings of Saint Thomas Aquinas*, II:433 [translation slightly modified]. On these questions, cf. Maritain, *Art et scolastique*, 26.
6. Thomas Aquinas, *Summa Theologiae*, Ia IIae, q. 57, a. 5; Pegis, *Basic Writings*, II:437.
7. Ibid.
8. Plotinus, *The Enneads*, V, 8, 1, and for the quotations that follow; tran. MacKenna, 411 [translations sometimes modified]. Cf. V, 9, 3; V, 9, 5; V, 9, 11.
9. Erwin Panofsky has written sentences on this topic that are not without ambiguity in *Idea: A Concept in Art Theory*, 28–31, 38. To begin with, the very project of culling from the ancient theory of art only that which concerns our "beaux-arts" and the "artist," whom the Ancients never distinguished from the artisan or craftsman, presents an act of indefensible violence and arbitrariness.
10. Plotinus, *The Enneads*, V, 8, 1; tran. MacKenna, 411 [translation modified].
11. Plotinus, *The Enneads*, III, 2, 16; tran. MacKenna, 152 [translation modified].
12. Plato, *Laws*, X, 892 B, in Cooper, *Plato, Complete Works*, 1549 [translation modified].
13. Plato will sometimes designate the intellectual forms with the word "nature."
14. Cicero, *De natura deorum*, L. II, chap. 22, §57–58, tran. Rackham, 177, 179 [translation modified].
15. Tertullian, *Apology, De Spectaculis*, XXI, 10; tran. Rendall, 107.
16. Cf. Scholem, *De la création du monde jusqu'à Varsovie*, 31–59. The disconcerting title, which is not the author's, takes nothing away from the quality of the great historian's analysis.
17. Augustine, *Eighty-three different Questions*, q. 78, tran. Mosher, *The Fathers of the Church*, 21:198.
18. Augustine, *De vera religione*, XXXVI, 67, in Burleigh, *Augustine: Earlier Writings*, 259.

19. Augustine, *De vera religione*, XXXVIII, 68; Burleigh, *Augustine: Earlier Writings*, 259.

20. Augustine, *De libero arbitrio*, II, 16, 43; tran. Russell, *The Teacher, The Free Choice of the Will, Grace and Free Will*, 59:152–53.

21. Focillon, *La vie des formes*, 4; tran. Hogan and Kubler, *The Life of Forms in Art*, 3 [translation modified].

22. Augustine, *De Trinitate*, VI, x, 11; tran. Hill, *The Trinity*, 213 [translation slightly modified].

23. Augustine, *De Civitate Dei*, XI, VII; tran. Dyson, *The City of God Against the Pagans*, 458 [translation slightly modified].

24. Augustine, *De Trinitate*, VIII, III, 5; tran. Hill, *The Trinity*, 245 [translation slightly modified].

25. Augustine, *In Evangelium Iohannis Tractatus*, I, 17, and likewise for the quotations that follow; tran. Rettig, *Tractates on the Gospel of John*, 56–57 [translation modified].

26. Rilke, *Duino Elegies*, 77.

27. Claudel, *Cinq grandes odes*, in *Œuvre poétique*, II:242–43.

28. Augustine, *In Evangelium Iohannis Tractatus*, XXXVII, 8; tran. Rettig, *Tractates on the Gospel of John*, 28–54 [translation modified].

29. Augustine, *De Civitate Dei*, XI, 29; tran. Dyson, *The City of God Against the Pagans*, 489.

30. Joubert, *Carnets*, 301.

31. Ibid., 214.

32. Ibid., 485, 775, 774.

33. Ibid., 467.

34. Ibid., 888.

35. Ibid., 758.

36. Ibid., 685: "In its strict meaning, man cannot be said to create in a good sense: we only create fantasies."

37. Ibid., 319.

38. Cf. Ibid., 487, and my study "Joseph Joubert: une philosophie à l'état naissant."

39. Eriugena, *Periphyseon*, III, 635 D-636 A, p. 64.

40. See on this point Beierwaltes, *Eriugena*, 146.

41. Eriugena, *Periphyseon*, II, 579 B-C, p. 120.

42. Ibid., 580 B, p. 120.

43. Ibid., 581 C-D, p. 126.

44. Cf. Beierwaltes, *Eriugena*, 150.

45. Anselm, *Monologion*, chap. XI.

46. Malebranche, *Méditations chrétiennes et métaphysiques*, XIX, 5, in *Œuvres complètes*, X, 217.

47. Bonaventure, *Breviloquium*, 2, 11, 2; tran. Vinck, *Works of Bonaventure*, II:102.

48. Ficino, *Theologia platonica*, XI, 5; *Théologie platonicienne*, II:129–30.

49. Ficino, *Theologia platonica*, XI, 5; *Théologie platonicienne*, II:133–34.

50. Ficino, *Theologia platonica*, XIII, 3; *Théologie platonicienne*, II:223.

51. Ibid., 224.

52. Ibid., 225; likewise for the following quotations.

53. Ibid., 226.

54. Ibid.

55. Cf. Leibniz, *Essais de théodicée*, III, §242; and Leibniz, *Monadologie*, §83–84.

56. Ficino, *Theologia platonica*, XIV, 1; *Théologie platonicienne*, II:246–47.

57. Cf. Ficino, *Theologia platonica*, XIV, 7; *Théologie platonicienne*, II:270–71.

58. Ficino, *Theologia platonica*, XIV, 4; *Théologie platonicienne*, II:260.

59. Ficino, *Theologia platonica*, XIV, 8; *Théologie platonicienne*, II:276.

60. Ficino, *Theologia platonica*, XIV, 9; *Théologie platonicienne*, II:279.

61. Nicholas of Cusa, *De venatione sapientiae*, IV, in Gabriel, *Philosophisch-theologische Schriften*, I:17.

62. Nicholas of Cusa, *De docta ignorantia*, L. II, XIII, in Gabriel, *Philosophisch-theologische Schriften*, I:410–16; tran. Hopkins, *Nicholas of Cusa, On Learned Ignorance*, 124.

63. Nicholas of Cusa, *Idiota de mente*, II, in Gabriel, *Philosophisch-theologische Schriften*, III:490.

64. Nicholas of Cusa, *Idiota de mente*, XIII, in Gabriel, *Philosophisch-theologische Schriften*, III:590–92.

65. Nicholas of Cusa, *De beryllo*, VI, in Gabriel, *Philosophisch-theologische Schriften*, III:8. Nicholas of Cusa transfers to *man* what the hermetic citation he makes at the beginning said in reality of the *world*.

66. Nicholas of Cusa, *Idiota de mente*, II, in Gabriel, *Philosophisch-theologische Schriften*, III:492.

67. Arthur Rimbaud to Paul Demeny, May 15, 1871, in *Œuvres complètes*, 251.

68. Heidegger, *Basic Writings*, 380.

69. Reverdy, "Les rêves monnayés," in *Main d'œuvre*, 9.

70. Reverdy, "Et maintenant," in *Main d'œuvre*, 533.

71. Ibid., 517. [Translator's note: *"Homme de main"* signifies a thug who does dirty work for a criminal boss; I later translate this expression with the English expression "strong-arm man." *"Homme de peine"* signifies a heavy-duty laborer; it can also mean "man of sorrow."]

72. Ibid., 390. [Translator's note: *"Main-morte"* means heavy-handed.]

73. Ibid., 432. [Translator's note: *"De la main à la main"* means, literally, from one hand to another, without intermediaries or formalities.]

74. Isidore of Seville, *Etymologiae*, XI, I, 66.

75. Paul Claudel to J. Madaule, letter, in Claudel and Madaule, *Connaissance et reconnaissance*, 128.

Like a Liquid Bond

JUST AS SOME, it is said, speak pearls, Paul Claudel speaks water. He speaks water without ceasing, and for this reason he has no need to be speaking of water all the time. And he certainly speaks water not with a mere trickle of a voice, but rather with a breath that is truly fluvial, hastening on to the far-off open sea that calls it forth. Water speaks, like us, because it listens, and like us tells because it sees. "I have a voice, and I listen, and I hear the sound that it makes. / And I make the water with my voice, water that is pure water, and, because it nourishes all things, all things paint themselves in it," says the second of the *Five Great Odes*, "The Spirit and the Water," before affirming that "The water that is clear sees with our eyes and, sonorous, hears with our ears. . . ."[1] There is water within us that is more intimate than ourselves, always more urgent than each of our fits of impatience. Tertullian, in his *De baptismo,* suddenly interrupts his fine description of the marvels of water to remind himself of his theological task, exclaiming: "I fear that I should be regarded as having gathered together the praises of water (*laudes aquae*) rather than the arguments for Baptism."[2] Never will the need to make such a choice cross Claudel's mind: he never saw such an alternative present itself, he never sought to contain, moderate, or dry up his own *laudes aquae*.

In the sequence mixing affection and ridicule that he wrote upon the death of Claudel, Francis Ponge compares him to a "dear old turtle":

> You will go off, diving to the other side of Asia,
> To swim in the hot seas of the Pacific,
> Like a great big sea turtle, our very own.
> What a weight you displace! And with such ease!
> What happiness amidst such gravity!

And he describes him flying through the water.[3] Yes, even if the drier wits may laugh, such is the very element of his speech, and his entire œuvre might be said to be "the great working phrase of water that proceeds on its single-minded duty."[4] Nowhere is he ever arid, and when in his prayer he reflects on his sins, he doesn't complain of dryness, but of water within him that has neither clarity nor life, water that lacks fluidity. "As for me, personally I regret only being able to offer as fuel this heavy water, this *thick water* of which the book of Maccabees speaks, this dirty liquid."[5]

Why these ever gushing, incessantly renewed *laudes aquae* in which poetry of water and mysticism of water inseparably sweep one another along and flow into one another? Is this all an imaginary, confused shimmering, an entirely subjective predilection for an element, with which any sort of psychology might nourish its *fascinatio nugacitatis?* Is it a theological metaphorics, the codes of which it would be necessary 'to inventory,' as it is said (as the *it* says in such a meaningless expression)? Must we refer it all back to the water ("e-a-u") doubly enclosed within a mirror and within a chiasmus in the name Paul Claudel, thus triply liquid? This would be to start adrift from the outset, and to ignore the things themselves, the water itself. It is clearly not the individual Paul Claudel who got it into his head to have a preference for water, but the divine Spirit who chose water to begin with, and it is not idiosyncrasy that gives a constant thirst for water to anyone reborn in it by baptism. Claudel's words of water do not emerge out of a private mythology, but are drawn from the "river of Scripture," from the "river of Revelation"[6]—they are biblical through and through. When he was in Brazil, Claudel writes, "I went through the Bible and I noted and accompanied with commentary all that the Holy Spirit, knowing what He says and what He does, despite what modern scholars say, tells us of the Waters. But I had to close up the work: I was submerged, rolled about, and carried off by the immensity and the splendor of the testimonies; perhaps one day I will again take up this gloss: this will be the work of my final years."[7] And this work was, in a certain way, accomplished, if we take into view the omnipresence of water in his exegetical writings, even if Claudel did not write a book on biblical waters.

A mystical poetry does not seek to be original, in the sense of inventive, but rather original in fidelity to the origin, and what it has to say that is most its own and most irreplaceable it says only by taking its place in the choir, or by speaking the most common language, which in this case is that of the Bible. Are we speaking here of a sort of symbolism? Indeed, Claudel will at times evoke "the immense symbolism of water."[8] But not without explicit reservations:

> How annoying it is to have to use the word *symbol!* It is a professorial term, it makes one believe that, between the sign and the thing signified, there is only a purely arbitrary and conventional resemblance, while there is a profound, essential kinship, and the two things were created in terms of one another, as if they owed their origin to the same word and there were a sort of continuity between the two.[9]

And those words, said with regard to water, lead several lines later to a meditation on "the beautiful river that flows between the two paradises, that of matter and that of the spirit, that of the senses and that of *sense*, this continual dialogue by means of image and reflection between the two banks of that which passes and that which lasts, of that which is and that which signifies."[10] If it is water itself that at the same time separates and unites the two banks, makes matter and spirit communicate without their merging, and marries senses and sense, giving the meaning to the senses and the senses to meaning, there is no metaphorics of water, because it is the condition and the possibility of all metaphor, of all passage and transport from the sensible to the spiritual and from the spiritual to the sensible, and its sacramental function, in a religion of the incarnation, renders the distinction of literal from figurative problematic. In *The Interior Castle*, Saint Teresa of Avila compares grace to water, writing: "For I don't find anything more appropriate to explain some spiritual experiences than water; and this is because I know little and have no helpful cleverness of mind and am so fond of this element that I have observed it more attentively than other things."[11] Claudel likes these sentences, which he cites on several occasions, recognizing himself in them.[12]

In speaking of water, Paul Claudel often begins with an undivided fluidity suitable to various manifestations that never forget their common source. An example is the page on which he distinguishes two elements in the physical and moral nature of man. The first is of stability, earth and flesh. "And there is another, fluid element, subtle, mobile, intelligent, penetrating, dynamic, and it is named, following the different figures that it takes, water, blood, breath, spirit. Following from this, the Apostle John writes: There are three things which give witness on the earth: the spirit and the water and the blood, and these three are one."[13] Water, blood, and spirit neither signify nor symbolize one another here; they converge, they conspire, they flow into one another in the unity of the same testimony, in a dynamic unity that is its very energy and mobility. Is it necessary to make explicit that the water in question is living water? "The water is nothing other than movement put at our disposal, which we must deliver to its destination." As for the water that has become "captive" and stagnant, the water that no longer moves and no longer circulates, it "corrupts itself and corrupts everything around it."[14] In the same way, he who stops the circulation of the water is doomed to the same corruption, for sin lies in immobilizing the water and the spirit that move, for example by refusing a cup of water to one who is thirsty.

This mobility of life could not stop itself on its own, for it is a *yes* to other forces, it is obedience made into an element. "Water, the element of life, the material that is the most narrowly associated with the spirit, the thing that is preeminently transparent and plastic to which there belongs only docility toward movement and transparency to the ray of light":[15] what is proper to water is thus to welcome the other or to yield to him, to have nothing for itself other than its suppleness and its ductility for the other. The inform is free for every form, its very weakness is rich with every strength. The waters, says Claudel again in one of his numerous lauds, "have by themselves no form or limit at all, and do not receive it unless it is imposed from outside. There is no exterior form that is proper to them, and which they tend to assume. They are preeminently *plastic*. . . . Like their limits, their divisions come from outside."[16] This pure, virgin future nevertheless remembers its origin, and its profusion, in the end, seeks unity. By its movement, the water goes toward the sea where it gathers into a "unique drop,"[17] and where its ἀπειρία becomes positive, and makes itself a figure of the inexhaustible and the infinite, "the very life without which everything is dead."[18]

> Ah! I haven't had enough! I look at the sea!
> All of it fills me, who am finite.
> But here and wherever I turn my face, and on this other side
> There is more, and again, and there too, and always and in
> the same way and even more! Always, dear heart!
> No reason to fear that my eyes might exhaust it.[19]

Concerning Thales of Miletus, who considered water the principle of all things in the world, the young Nietzsche wrote: "Thales saw the unity of being, and, when he wanted to communicate it, he spoke of water!"[20] In the same way, it might be said that, in seeing the unity of creation and the living circulation within it of the natural and the supernatural gifts of God, Claudel spoke of water, or indeed, spoke water. There is no paradox here, nor one word put in place of another, for water is at base the unique object of our desire, or rather, its unique interminable term. The extraordinary *Plan for an Underground Church in Chicago (Projet d'une Eglise souterraine à Chicago)* makes a principle of this desire for water: "All that the heart desires can always be reduced to the figure of water."[21]

If this is true, then thirst is the most proper name, and thus also the most mysterious one, for all desire. From the sinner to God himself, every being of desire is for Claudel a thirsty being. "I am thirsty!" says Doña Prouhèze to tell of her love, and Don Camille says: "Prouhèze, I believe in you! Prouhèze, I am dying of thirst!," and Prouhèze recalls for her guardian angel "the pitiless traction of thirst, the abomination of the frightful thirst that opens me up and crucifies me."[22] Just as much as the poems, the exegetical works never cease to cry out this thirst, and to make every being cry it out. "What good would it serve our soul to be a root, if there were nothing to serve as food for this capillary appetency that she is? Water, o my God! Open for us this *wellspring of living water that is your treasure.*"[23] We do not want to drink only with our mouths: the entire body with the soul, undivided, is thirst and calls for water, calls to the water that comes from God.

> *Sitio:* this is the cry of our beloved Savior on the cross! And we too, do we not die of thirst? . . . We die of thirst. . . . O my God, You have promised us water to drink, and that is enough! It is this water, and I do not know whether it is water or light, but even more water than light, it is this water in which I desire to drink and to plunge myself, to drink with my lungs and my entrails and my gills![24]

The naturalist Lacépède pompously established that fish have no thirst,[25] but for Claudel everything thirsts, even the Christian fish that we are; even water itself can be thirsty!

The desire for water is the desire for God. "How we desire water! Yes, between water and us there is a pact older than our life, and our soul desires, like an exiled deer yearns for eternal springs."[26] The poem "La route interrompue" concludes: "O Sea, how I desire you! and my soul, through everything within me that is humid I touch God!"[27] So alive, acute, so burning is this desire that the expression "a sea to swallow," far from referring for Claudel to an impossible and tedious task, as it does in everyday language, on the contrary designates what we

seek without ceasing until we find it. How should we
understand this? The second ode opposes the sea, as ultimate term of the desire for water, to the "arranged waters,"
"corruptible, flowing," where "the wellsprings are not at
all wellsprings." For we do not want just any water, we
want "the water itself," the complete and total water, "The
very element! / The primary matter! I say, it is the mother
that I need."[28] And clearly it is not a question of thirst here,
but of being at the sea's freedom and, within the sea, par-
ticipating in its communicative and irrepressible life, div-
ing into it, swimming in it, being free within the free
element. It is notable however that the poet opposes the sea
to "your drinkable waters," as if these are diminished in
being drinkable and apt to appease a thirst that would like
simply to drink, before comparing the sea to a more nour-
ishing and flavorful drink by speaking of the sea "with
entrails of grapes." All the same, in Claudel's work the
opposition between living water and dead water, pure
water and corrupted water, is more strongly present than
the opposition between fresh water and saltwater, between
drinkable water and undrinkable water.

Separated from Rodrigue by the diurnal Ocean, Doña
Prouhèze compares it to a cup from which, each from his
or her own side, they successively drink, and which, in the
evening, she hands to him when she has "drained" it. One
thus understands that drinking the sea that unites them
and keeps them apart can in no way suffice to appease her
thirst for her beloved.[29] But it is essentially within the mystical order that drinking the sea is at issue. If thirst is the
preeminent name for desire, and if the preeminent desire is
for the infinite God, there is finally no thirst but for the sea,
as image of the infinite. A page of commentary on the *Song
of Songs* shows this well, placing to the side the distinction
between fresh and saltwater. Evoking eternal life in which,
escaping from the desertlike dryness of death, "it will be
given to us to gulp to our heart's content at the Savior's
springs!" he immediately adds: "All I know is that, when I

open my eyes, this sea, for which the Infinite serves as limit, is not too much to be enough for my necessity."[30] Regarding the water of grace, *L'Evangile d'Isaïe*, in an amplification fitting to its object, passes from "a river" to "rivers," "rivers without any possibility of banks! . . . Do not think of the Yangtze or the Orenoco—think of the Gulf Stream!" The river becomes a river within the sea itself, a marine current.[31] But these analogies have the disadvantage of evoking an irreversible process, distancing itself ever more from its origin, while the tide suggests a going and a returning, which draws itself back only in order to return, like the very music of the world. "Thus the virtuoso who draws his bow its entire length, and then pushes it back out. The sea to drink? How nice! We needed nothing less to quench our thirst!"[32]

Considered in itself, this recurring expression "the sea to drink" might appear doubly inadequate to its object. On the one hand, it seems to name the desire for the Infinite in terms of what would instead be indefinite and ἄπειρον, the bad infinity of an always more, of pleonexia. On the other hand, it does not appear very Christian, if we remember Jesus' words to the Samaritan woman: "Whoever drinks of the water that I shall give him will never thirst."[33] But for Claudel the expression is more complex and richer than it first seems, and it does not confuse the infinite and the indefinite, as an astonishing page of commentary on the *Song of Songs* shows. "Someone placed me before the sea to drink, it was not too early, and I have only one thing to say: I am thirsty! I am thirsty, and someone brought me to drink a sea that is thirsty for me! Someone carried to my lips to drink a sea that is thirsty for me!"[34] What is this saying? This thirsty water is not an absurd and vain verbal game. According to Claudel's equivalence between desire and thirst, the water is thirsty because it desires. Certainly, "the water is the desired thing,"[35] and there is desire only for water, but it is also desire only through water, and water itself desires: "My God, have pity on these desiring waters!

. . . have pity on these waters in me that are dying of thirst!"[36] Water has thirst, because desire desires desire, and God is not a cup that fills us, but he who always already desires us, and has desired us, in order that we desire him, and desire him together, in desiring one another for him.

It is in this manner that Claudel understands the *Sitio*, the *I thirst* cried out by Christ upon the cross. The cry of the tortured Jesus is according to Claudel the point of incandescence of every desire and every thirst in creation. First and last, it proclaims their meaning. God and man, he makes divine thirst and human thirst encounter and evoke one another. Thus the *Evangile d'Isaïe* recalls the eschatological chapter of Matthew, where it is said: "I was thirsty, and you gave me to drink": "*Thirst?* and of what other than thirst? the thirst of all these mouths to which I was delivered, like a spring."[37] This thirst of Jesus is nothing other than the torn, rent violence of his life for those he wants to bring back to God, which is to say, everyone. In *Un poète regarde la Croix,* Claudel opposes the fourth word of Christ on the cross to pagan morality, which tends toward the moderation or "suppression of desire." And this thirst becomes the very meaning of the world. "God has thirst only for God. The Son of God has appentency only for His Father, and Man, representative of all the creatures, essentially thirsts only for his Author. But below Him God, in the entire creation, thirsts for that which is of Him, for that which is for Him, for that which is addressed to Him."[38] The term thirst is thus applied here as much to intradivine or Trinitarian relations as to the relation of man and, through him, all things to God, and to the relation of God to creation. The most carnal desire, the most common and banal carnal desire, also forms the name of the most spiritual desire. All of this is grounded in what theology calls the communication of properties: the incarnation of God authorizes the usage of the same word for orders that metaphysics would carefully distinguish.

The thirst for thirst figures this circularity of life, which comes from God and goes toward Him. Is it so strange that water itself could have thirst, if water is preeminently, for Claudel, the power of mobility, the very direction of meaning and toward meaning, and if thirst names the desire that continually disturbs and propels? And thirst, like a burning, is transmitted from God to man and from man to God like water itself; the circle of thirst and the circle of water are the same, a circle of desire. Several pages after this sublime evocation of universal thirst, Claudel speaks, just as magnificently, of the circulation of water. The "virtue of water, in some sense invitatory and provocative," links it to the clever desire to go to meet its object, inventing by any means the paths that lead there. Water "is this secret sap that seeks all the elements that are capable of constructing in a single body the child of God," the mystical body of Christ, the universal Church. "It clears ways for itself that are known to Him alone."[39] Water "is the universal preliminary contact" by the creator with the creation, the call that makes the creation be by stretching it or directing it toward him, and water for Claudel becomes, audaciously, the very thing by which God knows—and knows by tasting—the world: "it is by [water] that the author of all matter procures for himself a sapid knowledge of it."[40]

Yes, we want the sea to drink, for the thirst that is ours exceeds the measure of man, it is within us greater and more ardent than we are, it is desire for God. This is why one can and must give thanks for this thirst. "I thank you, Lord, who gave me a thirst that measures up to my swallowing! And what human by his own strength would be capable of doing justice to this prodigious brim-full! . . . This spirit in us that cries *Abba:* what other than the Father who is your Father would be capable of satisfying it?"[41] And, in his commentary on the *Song of Songs,* Claudel, evoking once again God who "thirsts for our thirst," wonders about "this astonishing cooperation between the Creator and his creature": "It is God in me who is the desirer, it is God who is the desired, it is God who is the desire."[42] But this circle does not make us disappear, does not evaporate us as if, in front of the absolute glory of the Absolute, we were only an ephemeral dream, as if the Creator would want to dissolve his creation; for this is the circle that raises us to our highest dignity and to our clearest strength by allowing us to participate endlessly in his life. This is why thirst—the thirst for justice—forms part of the Beatitudes: what God "asks of His servants" (and we know that He alone gives what He asks for) "is not to stop thirsting with Him. What He promises them is to furnish them with what they need to be ever blessedly thirsty with Him!"[43] Claudel wants only an inextinguishable thirst.

The thirst for thirst is a name for charity: it is the thirst that water has to spill and to spread itself. If the desire we have for God is in us, thanks to him, and in every way exceeds us and blessedly tears us open, it is older within us than we ourselves. Thirst, which is our very vocation, makes us go ever further forward, it calls us to the future, a future beyond human measures and calculations, and yet it has something immemorial about it, for that which exceeds us precedes us. This gives meaning to certain of Claudel's words, which would otherwise remain enigmatic. If the desire for God is our vocation, and in a sense the telluric work within us of this vocation, it has presided over our very creation, and the water that at the same time fills and elicits in us this desire is for us more intimate and older than we ourselves. The water that we are, the water that flows in us, through us, and via us, remembers its source before remembering itself. Thus Claudel, in a page already cited, can affirm rigorously: "Between water and us there is a pact older than our life,"[44] because the waters always already are, and the Spirit always already moves over them; because its originary bond with the waters was never broken, and in every moment remains alive, as at the beginning.[45]

Just as water has something immemorial about it, so too does speech. To speak of water is not to begin speaking by breaking the very first silence, but to carry water to the already existing sea, which, contrary to the intention of the proverb, is far from being a vain activity. The second ode is presented to God, with the evocation of verses from Genesis, "Not at all like a thing that begins, but little by little like the sea that was there, / The sea of all human words" . . . , even though it is a "new Ode."[46] And when, in his commentary on the *Song of Songs*, Claudel has the Virgin Mary give an invitation to tears—tears of penitence, tears of joy, tears of love—he has her conclude her address with these words: "Allow, allow this origin within you that slowly awakens to benefit from this pact that I have made with the sea."[47] An originary pact, for Claudel sees in the sea of Genesis (*Congregationes aquarum appellavit Maria*) the figure of Mary, Maria. Mary is a "spring" too, "she is there, and there is something future in us, older than us, which exults, and which has chosen the sun."[48]

Water is thus doubly eschatological: it concerns the extremities of time, the origin and the end, the Genesis and the Apocalypse. From water we come, and we go toward water. Claudel sometimes even takes the risk of deciphering sacred history in geography and hydrology, reading time in space, with the rivers as "essential directions": "Do you thus mean to say that all the waters of the earth have as a memory that guides them a sort of former paradise?"[49] And Claudelian physiology makes us relive in our very body, thanks to liquid, the foundational events, linking water and the time of origins, of perpetual origins. The blood that bathes the heart is not only thought, as it was for Empedocles;[50] it is also memory, a memory that is more essential than every conscious act of recollection. Thus we have our inner Easter, at once spiritual and corporal.

> The Sea, the Red Sea, is our blood, now considered in its circulation (and thus these are the rivers), and now considered in terms of the whole of this vital liquid in which we are bathed. . . . It is through our blood that we must clear a way. . . . We go as far as the Promised Land through nothing other than flesh and blood.[51]

All of this prepares us to understand why the tie between creatures and God can be, in the second ode, named "a liquid bond." Fluid as the expression may be, it is not any less paradoxical, for, while one says that a river connects two cities or two regions by allowing circulation and commerce by way of water, is it not the case that a bond that would not be solid, that would not bind solidly, a bond that flows, breaks free and goes away, a bond that does not remain the same for a single instant, a bond that one cannot hold between one's fingers—doesn't such a bond seem evanescent? "Thus water continues the spirit, and supports it, and feeds it/And between/All your creatures up to you there is something like a liquid bond."[52] This liquid bond, which is circulation, flux, the incessant and always renewed excess of desire that we have for God, and that God has for us, is that by which "all the bonds are explained and resolved";[53] it is the bond that unbinds,[54] the bond that delivers, the bond that softens all that is hardened and frozen, the very bond of the voice that calls and responds.

This bond is also the bond of blood. Indeed, Claudel will employ the expression "liquid bond" on at least two other occasions in his exegetical works, always applied to the relation of creatures to God. And, in the two cases in question, this will be to speak about blood. In *Un poète regarde la Croix,* while pondering the relation of the soul and of blood, and the Old Testament instruction "not to mix flesh and blood," he writes: "God follows, so to speak, that blood of which He, within us, is the inspirer, that liquid bond which ties Him to us."[55] In the living body blood is the "divine sap," God's part. And, in the commentary on the *Song of Songs,* while addressing himself to the Virgin Mary, Claudel writes:

> Explain to us this heart, this flesh that you made for him, connect us up with His divinity by all of the fibers of our human sensibility. But no textile comparisons! this is about something else! this is about a liquid bond, about the connecting of arteries and veins, about heartbeats . . . , it is

about a mobilization of my substance for His sake . . . , at our very depths it is about the general opening of our valvules due to the inrush of the spiritual stream.[56]

The "liquid bond" is vital and dynamic; it renews and regenerates itself at each moment, as in a continual creation, a promise made anew.

Thus we understand that for Claudel, sin, or the rupture and distance between man and God, between human and divine life, results from "accidents of circulation,"[57] circulation of the spirit, of water or of blood, which are one. He feigns to "excuse" himself for "constantly mixing the language of the body with that of the soul"[58]—feigns, indeed, because right away to do it he bases himself upon Scripture itself, which does not have to be justified. And in any case mixture is not the correct term, because the issue is rather a perpetual exchange and a circulation where the spirit is incorporated and the body becomes spiritual. Claudel's physiology is through and through theological, and his theology is unceasingly incarnated and incorporated: it is in this that it is most profoundly and most rigorously Christian. In the work of Claudel there can never be a question concerning God, nor our relation to God, nor the relation of God to us, without the Incarnation of God in Christ being present as at once both the center and the horizon of this word.

The "secularized universe" is for Claudel that in which the "holy movement of nature," across which the spirit circulates and gives witness to its origin, is interrupted. It forms nothing more than "a puddle that decays." The waters are no longer living, everything goes to death and toward death, following an entropy that dries up and asphyxiates. The "interior liquidity" of things, which is an integral part of their availability, has been lost.[59] There is in all of this not the least bit of "naturalism" in the theological sense of the term: our "liquid bond" to God requires that the body, "complete in the integrity of its members and of its organs," must "be evangelized."[60] And indeed, Claudel never stops evangelizing the circulation of the

unknown blood of the Bible and of the Church Fathers.
For the "liquid bond" is a rhythmic bond: "Return to the
source! Beat with Me."[61]

The identity of blood and water is a central thesis in
Claudel's physiology. In *The Sword and the Mirror (L'épée et le
miroir)*, he gives in an appendix a list of scriptural texts that
treat water in its diverse forms (sea, rivers, streams, dew),
under the title: "Texts on the Circulation of Blood."[62] This
altogether explicit identity is affirmed many times: "What is
blood? . . . It is the interior water laden with knowledge and
spirit which, each second, weighs and counts our entire
body, detaches from it the worn-out elements, and draws
upon the altar of our lungs, maintained by this incessant
inflow, a luminous fire that bears to the ensemble of our
organs the unifying pulse of life."[63] Directly or indirectly,
Claudel made the notion of an interior milieu, formed by
Claude Bernard, his own, and evangelized it.

Must we see in what Bachelard called a "poetics of living
blood" an idiosyncrasy of the Claudelian imagination?[64]
This would be botchery as much as nescience. For if water
constitutes the name of the liquid element of which all the
liquids are simply modes, declining this element according
to various functions, it is cosmologically inevitable that
blood is water. The Dogons, if we are to believe Marcel
Griaule, affirm this also, like some sort of African Thales:
"The vital strength of the earth is water. God molded the
earth with water. Similarly, he makes blood with water.
Even in stone there is this strength, because humidity is in
everything."[65] And the circulation of blood, once discov-
ered, lends itself so well to the analogy of blood and water
that Descartes, in the treatise on *L'homme* in which he
expounds his mechanistic physiology, finds nothing more
clear and distinct to illustrate the functioning of the body
than a hydraulic comparison. In the fountains, he writes,
"that are in the gardens of our Kings, . . . the sole force by
which the water moves, in exiting from its source, is suffi-
cient to move various machines." Thus it is for the body

itself. The nerves are comparable to pipes, the muscles to springs, and "the animal spirits, to the water that moves them, of which the heart is the source, and the concavities of the brain the manholes" (in the sense of what plumbers call an inspection hatch). Breathing and other bodily functions are "like the movements of a clock, or of a mill, which the regular flow of water can render continuous." And Descartes finishes by assimilating the reasonable soul that is in this machine to the "water engineer, who must be in the inspection hatches where all the pipes connect."[66]

Thus, what characterizes the body for Claudel is not this identification of blood and water, which we could also find in Leonardo da Vinci and many other authors, but the conviction that the body is not a machine, even if it has its mechanisms and its hydraulics, and that the water engineer is God himself. The "burning and luminous" blood is also the Word that flows in us and comes to make us live. "This plastic liquid, this holy wave whose regular stream with each throb of the central pump never stops building us, cleaning us, and verifying us,"[67] this blood that passes through the "isthmus" of the neck,[68] is the *incorporation* of sacred history, and a sort of Genesis in motion, always and forever. The circulation of blood, "vehicle of the soul," is this "essential movement that witnesses to he who was breathed into us by the Prime Mover." It constitutes the surety that "the spirit in us, as in the beginning, continues to be borne upon the waters,"[69] as Claudel likes to repeat, describing the world just as much as our bodies. Elsewhere, Claudel assimilates our bodies to Paradise, with its rivers.[70] And within us, blood is a sea, "salted by Wisdom," a sea, "this fluid ambiance which constitutes our interior milieu, in exchange with and in continual contact with the exterior milieu."[71] And if every word is uttered only to be understood, "that is the function of this heart in me that I hear continually in the midst of stirring up its sea, in the midst of inhaling everything, in the midst of proposing all or obliging all to communication."[72]

In the homage he wrote at the death of Paul Claudel, Saint-John Perse recalled a walk he took with him in 1912, during which Claudel "suddenly, as if for himself, made this great land-lover's remark: 'The sea . . . the sea, that's the future life.'"[73] The entirely rigorous meaning of this phrase is not that which Perse seems to attribute to it. For it is true that for Claudel the promise of eternity is maritime. He has Christ say: "I have come to bring you the horizon, I have come to bring you the sea."[74] Our life of grace goes from water to water, from the water of the river to the water of the sea: "The Euphrates, *this great river . . .* , is baptism. The Promised Land extends between this sacramental frontier and the sea, which is Eternity."[75] The ultimate identity of the sky and the sea is such that Claudel, in an unexpected manner, comes to compare the wings of the seraphim "to fins and gills."[76] And the fish that, because of its Greek name, was the image of Christ and a sign among Christians, is also the figure of what, at the resurrection, we are called to become: our bodies will be the same as they are here, but "the same to the waters, henceforward fish of another abode," says the *Ode jubilaire* for Dante.[77]

All of these evocations, at first strange and disconcerting, are based upon a biblical and theological meditation on the *higher waters.* The separation of water from water forms the second of God's acts of creation, after the separation of light from darkness. It is the work of the second day: "And God made the firmament and separated the waters which were under the firmament from the waters which were above the firmament."[78] These higher waters, these waters situated above the firmament, elicit, in theology as much as in cosmology, many questions, difficulties, and speculations, as we can see in the numerous commentaries on the book of Genesis. Claudel was haunted by these higher waters, and presented an interpretation as profound and beautiful as it is risky. They are not the waters that we find here, even though these waters are the image and, as it were, the natural and analogical foretaste of the higher waters. The higher waters are heaven itself, in the theological sense—the site of eternal life, to which we are promised.

> Thus let us call them: *The Waters*, and in so doing we will do nothing more than follow the example of all the Seers of the Old and New Testaments, this intermediate and living element whose existence we envision between God and man, and of which the Psalmist tells us that *they have seen God*, and which he commands to *praise the Lord.*[79]

These waters would be a state of matter, but a state that is distinct from that which we know, "a state of explosion, of liberty, of effusion, of discharge, of surging, of welling up."[80]

The water poured over us at baptism is only a "prelibation" of these higher waters, where we will be eternally. "Since they have taken our souls, they are thirsty for our bodies."[81] This is why Claudel can write with a tone of self-evidence in his *Projet d'une Eglise souterraine à Chicago* that "Water . . . principally signifies Heaven."[82] For, as he says elsewhere, Heaven is "the perfectly limpid and bare creature, the perfectly supple vehicle, the perfectly docile revealer, the perfectly translucent excipient"; there "we are entirely wet and submerged," and with Heaven "everything stays in contact."[83] This fluid milieu allows beings to be together perfectly, to be in unity without merging into one another, to communicate unreservedly without dissolving into this gift itself. The water-heaven or the heaven-water transmits movement and sonority. It is, in the etymological sense, the cordial element, that of the heart. In *The Satin Slipper (Le soulier de satin)*, the tide forms "the pulse of the beating world,"[84] but the sea also communicates the pulse of men. When Sept-Epées swims with the butcher's wife, who nevertheless will drown, she evokes "this sort of liquid light, which makes us into . . . glorified bodies," and proclaims: "Directly with my heart I feel each beat of your heart."[85] The element comprises us, surrounds us in every way, and comprises us together, making it so that we can be for one another, all for God, in a perfect and distinct intimacy. There is something catholic about the ocean according to Claudel.

His beautiful meditation on "the place and condition of resurrected bodies" (the manuscript of which was destroyed, ironically, by fire) describes the "pacific waters" of eternal life. Through this medium, "through this torrent of living and delicate light in which we will be immersed, we will all, so to speak, be leaning on Christ . . . and we will count each of the beatings of his heart, we will have contact directly with him."[86] Commenting on the first three days of Genesis, Claudel says that, in these higher Waters, "the palpitation of each being is associated with that of all the others."[87] We will be "like fish."[88] If it is true that, as Claudel says, "several fathers" of the Church liken these higher Waters to Heaven,[89] they do so rather to resolve the cosmological difficulties elicited by their existence than to describe the eternal life that awaits us there. For Claudel, in contrast, these waters that are not water are, yet again, water, by a sort of reversal of the final myth of Plato's *Phaedo*. For Plato, we are only like fish with regard to the inhabitants of the higher Earth, for the sea is associated with imperfection and corruption, while for Claudel our ultimate future is to become like fish in a higher Sea. The communion of saints will be maritime.

Thus it is not through a merely fortuitous image that Claudel can identify the sea with the future life. The "liquid bond" that unites the creature with the creator, and through the creator the creatures with one another, is at the same time original and ultimate. It precedes and follows human life in its present condition, and never ceases to sustain it and to accompany it all along its laborious history. We come from water and we go toward water, being ourselves water, and the word in us never finishes flowing, listening to and responding to the eternal bubbling of the divine Word. This is why, recalling the words of a psalm,[90] and substituting a spring for the sea, Claudel writes: "One hand on the spring and one hand on the rivers!" The right hand "executes" and the other "possesses." "This is eternity under its two aspects, the infinite and the inexhaustible, permanence and activity."

"Happy is he who thus deepens within himself this particular image of God in which he was constituted."[91] The "poem of the Sea" that Rimbaud spoke of is for Claudel a mystical poem, of a mysticism of the incarnation.

NOTES

1. Claudel, *Œuvre poétique*, 242–43.
2. Tertullian, *De baptismo*, I, 6; tran. Souter, *Tertullian's Treatises*, 49.
3. Ponge, *Le grand recueil, Lyres*, 32–33.
4. Claudel, *Un poète regarde la Croix*, 271; cf. Claudel, *Les aventures de Sophie*, 185.
5. Claudel, *Un poète regarde la Croix*, 287.
6. Claudel, *Introduction au livre de Ruth*, 59–60.
7. Claudel, *Paul Claudel interroge l'Apocalypse*, 235.
8. Claudel, *Œuvres complètes*, XV:198.
9. Claudel, *Au milieu des vitraux*, 57.
10. Ibid., 57–58.
11. Teresa of Avila, *The Interior Castle* IV, 2, 2:385; tran. Kavanaugh and Rodriguez, *The Collected Works of St. Teresa of Avila*, 2:323.
12. Cf. Claudel, *Au milieu des vitraux*, 57; Claudel, *Journal*, t. I, p. 942.
13. Claudel, *Un poète regarde la Croix*, 266. Claudel quotes from the Vulgate. The Greek has: οἱ τρεῖς εἰς τό ἕν εἴσιν. Claudel frequently cites this text from I John 5:8.
14. Claudel, *Un poète regarde la Croix*, 267. Cf. Claudel, *Œuvre poétique*, 666.
15. Claudel, *Au milieu des vitraux*, 47.
16. Claudel, *Œuvres complètes*, XXVIII:268.
17. Claudel, *Œuvre poétique*, 237.
18. Ibid., 236.
19. Ibid. Cf. Claudel, *L'Evangile d'Isaïe*, 109.
20. Nietzsche, *Œuvres philosophiques complètes*, I, pt. 2, 224.
21. Claudel, *Œuvres complètes*, XV:198. Gaston Bachelard commented on this sentence in his book *L'eau et les rêves*.
22. Claudel, *Le soulier de satin*, III:8, 10, 8, respectively, in *Théâtre*, II:812, 842, 821.

23. Claudel, *L'Evangile d'Isaïe*, 196.

24. Claudel, *Paul Claudel interroge l'Apocalypse*, 233.

25. "The fluid in which fish are submerged can thus . . . preserve them from this painful sensation that has been called thirst, which originates in the dryness of the mouth and of the alimentary canal, and which, consequently, must never exist in the midst of water." Lacépède, *Histoire naturelle*, I:476.

26. Claudel, *Au milieu des vitraux*, 57.

27. Claudel, *Œuvre poétique*, 696.

28. Ibid., 236.

29. Claudel, *Le soulier de satin*, III:8, in *Théâtre*, II:812.

30. Claudel, *Cantique des cantiques*, 174.

31. Cf. Claudel, *Paul Claudel interroge l'Apocalypse*, 241.

32. Claudel, *L'Evangile d'Isaïe*, 109–10.

33. John 4:14.

34. Claudel, *Cantique des cantiques*, 443–44.

35. Claudel, *Œuvre poétique*, 244.

36. Ibid. In *L'eau et les rêves* (77), Bachelard misunderstood the full significance of this expression because he did not see the connection with desire.

37. Claudel, *L'Evangile d'Isaïe*, 295. Cf. 158, regarding the *Sitio:* "Not only a thirsty root: a root of thirst!"

38. Claudel, *Un poète regarde la Croix*, 125–26.

39. Ibid., 130.

40. Ibid., 131–32.

41. Claudel, *Paul Claudel interroge l'Apocalypse*, 239.

42. Claudel, *Cantique des cantiques*, 403–4.

43. Claudel, *La rose et le rosaire*, 245–46.

44. Claudel, *Au milieu des vitraux*, 57.

45. Claudel, *La rose et le rosaire*, 214–15.

46. Claudel, *Œuvre poétique*, 235.

47. Claudel, *Cantique des cantiques*, 288.

48. Ibid., 290.

49. Claudel, *Au milieu des vitraux*, 53.

50. Diels and Kranz, *Die Fragmente der Vorsokratiker* B, 105, 1:350.

51. Claudel, *Cantique des cantiques*, 353–54.

52. Claudel, *Œuvre poétique*, 241.

53. Ibid., 247.

54. Cf. Ibid., 237: "the water that has made the earth unbinds it."

55. Claudel, *Un poète regarde la Croix*, 266–67.

56. Claudel, *Cantique des cantiques*, 296–97.
57. Claudel, *Œuvres complètes*, XXVIII:29. Cf. Claudel, *Au milieu des vitraux*, 47.
58. Claudel, *Cantique des cantiques*, 331–32.
59. Claudel, *Au milieu des vitraux*, 146.
60. Claudel, *Cantique des cantiques*, 333.
61. Claudel, *L'épée et le miroir*, 235.
62. Ibid., 229.
63. Claudel, *Au milieu des vitraux*, 47.
64. Bachelard, *L'eau et les rêves*, 84.
65. Griaule, *Dieu d'eau*, 17.
66. Descartes, *Œuvres philosophiques*, I:390–91.
67. Claudel, *Cantique des cantiques*, 326.
68. Ibid., 327.
69. Ibid., 134–35.
70. Ibid.
71. Claudel, *Au milieu des vitraux*, 145. Cf. Claudel, *Œuvres complètes*, XXVIII:30.
72. Claudel, *Cantique des cantiques*, 352.
73. Perse, "Silence pour Paul Claudel," 390.
74. Claudel, *Introduction au livre de Ruth*, 107.
75. Claudel, *Paul Claudel interroge l'Apocalypse*, 114.
76. Claudel, *La rose et le rosaire*, 44.
77. Claudel, *Œuvre poétique*, 686.
78. Gen. 1:7.
79. Claudel, *Paul Claudel interroge l'Apocalypse*, 235.
80. Ibid., 234.
81. Claudel, *Œuvres complètes*, XXVIII:241.
82. Ibid., XV:298.
83. Ibid., XXVIII:240–41.
84. Claudel, *Le soulier de satin*, IV:6, in *Théâtre*, II:907.
85. Claudel, *Le soulier de satin*, IV:10, in *Théâtre*, II:938.
86. Claudel, *Œuvres complètes*, XXVIII:255.
87. Ibid., 269–70.
88. Ibid., 254.
89. For more details than Claudel offers, cf. Suárez, *Opera omnia*, III:111.
90. Ps. 89:25.
91. Claudel, *Cantique des cantiques*, 210.

Elementary Tears

THAT WHICH BREAKS the voice by interrupting the stream of its words still belongs to it. Such is the case with tears, which speak without naming anything, without saying anything, in the pure effusion of meaning. We are no longer the masters of this meaning; it passes through us to give itself and lose itself. At the peak of this trembling glimmer, at the very height of tears and their effacement, there would be weeping without knowing that one weeps; we would not even let our tears flow, as if we were still making a decision to cry or not, nor would we any longer weep out of sadness or out of joy, but instead simply weep sadness or joy—weep in the oblivion of our weeping. Thus perhaps our tears, in truly giving way, would gather in themselves the sadness or the joy of that which cannot weep, and it would be the world that shines in their ephemeral crystal.

Are there tears that belong to no one, tears without anyone who weeps? Sometimes on window panes the cloud of vapor ceases to be a veil that is flat, even, and somnolent in the indefinite clarity, and instead, as it carries on the effort of its condensation, animating itself into coalescence, animating itself with coalescence, it begins to form tears. It is beautiful that they express nothing—it removes all limitation and all imitation from them. We speak commonly of a face *veiled* by tears, which is not true: a face can be twisted with fear, spite, rage, or disappointment, but what is more unbearably naked than a face in tears? As to the streaming of tears on window panes: it opens days, arranges cracks of light as hazardous as they are precise, allows a glimpse of that which an instant before was hidden. When the panes weep, the world is purer.

The Czech photographer Josef Sudek left behind a body of work in which the poetics of the window takes on its full intensity. A poetics of the window, but also of the pane, of the clouded pane. At issue here is not simply a journey around his room, but an immobile journey across this vaporous and peacefully lachrymal veil. Sudek photographs branches, trees, barred fences, and houses, each glimpsed from the window of his studio. The focus is on that which veils, the cloud upon the pane of glass, and what one glimpses behind this veil reinforces its indefiniteness. Sometimes, these are only incoordinate fragments. But at other times, the landscape, instead of dissolving into evanescence and blur, is simplified into masses worthy of an energetic charcoal drawing, and takes on a paramnesic force of affirmation, as if we had already seen these trees and these houses, as if we too lived day in day out in front of them and with them.

Because the frames and sills of the windows do not appear, but only the pane, with its tears tracing their streaks sometimes darker, sometimes lighter, the pane itself becomes like a photographic plate, a photograph to the second power. The minute precision that the vapor confers upon the vision of the plane of the glass gives the photograph a certain mural-like aspect, and the depth beyond that is guessed at is denied as much as affirmed. Does the clouded pane show us a fragment of landscape become simpler and more sober, or is it rather the cloud that shows us the pane, which is to say, shows us that which normally one does not see? The pane of glass itself becomes the site where light and shadows write themselves, and it manifests itself as such. The means of vision becomes the object of vision. And, in certain of Josef Sudek's shots, he alone is given to be seen.

The relations of interior and exterior are thus powerfully disturbed. As a general rule, the function of a pane of glass is at the same time to unite and to distinguish interior and exterior: it allows being inside and outside all at once, seeing the exterior while remaining in the interior. The vapor veils this transparency, makes a curtain of the pane, and thus, in a certain way, closes the interior upon itself. But in Sudek's work, nothing of this interior space appears, not even a sill or a frame, and the interior is no longer a dwelling place, but only a wide-open gaze, pure vision. And the veiled exterior, glimpsed with difficulty, is laden with a patient, slow secret. Hasn't the exterior become intimate, while the interior is no more than a gaze outside of itself, passed entirely into what it sees? Sudek shows tears that unveil, tears belonging to no one upon the humble surface of windowpanes.[1] These are not yet elementary tears, cosmic tears. Is there such a thing?

Il pleure dans mon cœur   It weeps in my heart
Comme il pleut sur la ville. As it rains on the town.

Thus begins, as we all remember, the third of Verlaine's *Ariettes oubliées (Forgotten Ariettas),* from the beginning of *Romances sans paroles (Songs Without Words).*[2] In this poem, which persists in and insists upon its own effacement by making words rhyme with themselves and sometimes even with nothing, according to the repetition of ennui that seems almost uninterruptible, what is most admirable is this initial impersonal verb of tears: *"Il pleure,"* taken up again in the third quatrain by an *"Il pleure sans raison,"* "It weeps without cause." It is raining in me like it is raining in the space of the world, it is raining in me without my crying, it is raining tears unspilled, as if being on the verge of tears had lost its imminence, and had become a state in which to stand, to hold oneself, to be undone, within oneself more than from one's self, *"dans ce cœur qui s'écœure,"* "in this heart-sick heart." Rain of tears, tears of rain, each being called the other, without truly meeting, without having to meet, so much are they interdependent from the outset.

Has anyone noticed that, without there being a true ending, the poem ends with the renunciation of knowing what, in the Roman rite prior to Vatican II, the priest asked at the beginning of the Mass, before climbing to the altar, *"Quare*

tristis es, anima mea, et quare conturbas me?" (Why are you
sad, o my soul, and why do you trouble me?), just prior to
exhorting himself to hope in God and to praise him?

C'est bien la pire peine	'Tis surely the worst woe
De ne savoir pourquoi	To know not wherefore
Sans amour et sans haine	My heart suffers so
Mon cœur a tant de peine.	Without joy or woe.

This woe at the "without a why" of woe corresponds to
the inward tears of the absence of tears. These tears without a subject, without belonging, without cause, make
common cause with the sadness of the world: these are the
tears of the world that fall within me.

This analogy, or chiasmus, of rain and tears belonged as
well to earlier poetry. For instance, Guillaume du Bartas, in
his poetic heptameron *La semaine ou la création du monde
(The Divine Weeks, First Week)*, describes the wind that, "by
many sighs" *(par mainte soupir)*, shakes "tears" from the
clouds, before evoking a more violent downpour in which

Lors maint fleuve céleste en nos fleuves se perd
On ne voit rien que pleurs.

The mighty celestial river is swallowed up by our rivers
And one sees nothing but tears.[3]

Here too, these tears are those of no one; the lines
describe the tears of the world. During the Middle Ages,
Hildegard of Bingen, in her splendid and strange anthro-
pological cosmology or cosmological anthropology,
described in a strictly parallel fashion the formation of rain
in the world and that of tears in the human body.[4] But it
must be added that the tears of which she speaks are just as
much tears of joy as of sadness.

In a prose text to which Bachelard drew attention,
Lamartine goes to the limit and sees in water itself, gener-
ally speaking, "the sad element." Evoking Psalm 137,
where the exiles weep by the waters of Babylon, which
inspired one of Johann Sebastian Bach's most sublime

chorales, Lamartine adds: "Why? Because the water weeps along with everyone."[5] It weeps upon our cheeks as it weeps in the rivers. The watercourse is effusion. It ceaselessly accomplishes what language says in speaking of "melting into tears," as if we, being nothing more than sadness, wanted to disappear into our very tears, and be nothing more than the act, if it is an act, of weeping without end: the weeper is no longer separated nor distinct from her tears, she goes along weeping, and weeps while going along with the same movement of surrender.

Victor Hugo assigns this role to the sea, without thereby exhausting all its possibilities, for clearly the sea also has its joy. In the storm, "one hears the sob of creation. The sea is the great weeper. She is laden with moans; the ocean laments for everything that suffers."[6] But isn't the oceanic moan, where the sea rolls its own flood of tears up and down, just as much, if not more, that of the wind than of the water? The violent union of the two elements of air and water is what heaves forth this clamor for the calamity and distress of the living. This irritable and violent-tempered moan does not make the sea itself "the sad element."

Alfred de Musset, at the beginning of his poem *Rolla*, sees in the sea's tears a beneficent and generative power. He evokes the time of the pagan theogony:

> Où Vénus Astarté, fille de l'onde amère,
> Secouait, vierge encore, les larmes de sa mère,
> Et fécondait le monde en tordant ses cheveux.

> Where Venus Astarte, daughter of the bitter wave,
> Shook off, while still a virgin, the tears of her mother,
> And impregnated the world by winding her hair.[7]

This fleeting and learned allusion neither lingers over nor ponders the elementary. The fact that these tears in the end become so joyous in their effect emerges rather from a witticism. In the passage from Hesiod that inspired Musset, there is in no sense whatsoever talk of tears, but rather of the generosity of Aphrodite.

As for the Manicheans, they on the contrary see in nature the rending passion of the imprisoned spirit: plants suffer when they are uprooted, and bread, the very bread with which we sustain our lives, spills tears when it is cut: *Credunt panem plorare* (they believe that bread weeps), says Saint Augustine, who rightly remarks that this amounts to "twisting the human feeling of mercy toward who knows what delirious cruelties."[8] What a bitter taste a tortured, tearful loaf of bread must have!

More significant than these scattered references are two ancient myths that make of the sea itself, indeed of all the water in the world, a tear. The first is confirmed by some Pythagorean expressions and commented upon by Plutarch in relation to certain Egyptian beliefs, in his treatise on Isis and Osiris; the second is gnostic, from the Valentinian sect, and is reported to us by Church Fathers like Saint Irenaeus of Lyon, as well as by Tertullian. The Pythagoreans named the sea a "tear of Kronos." *Kronou dakruon:* this strange and beautiful expression is cited by Saint Clement of Alexandria as an example of Pythagorean allegories, and Porphyry, taking it from a lost work of Aristotle, evokes it among others as a sample of the teaching that Pythagoras "delivered in a mysterious manner in the form of symbols."[9] Yet neither the meaning of this mystery nor the content of this teaching are ever indicated. Kronos, who castrated his father, imprisoned his brothers, and ate his children, did not leave the memory of a marked penchant for sentimentality. Is this a tear of sadness, of spite, or of anger? Nothing about it is said.

The sole explanation is given by Plutarch, in the midst of a vast development, but the form of his sentence manifests that for him this is only conjecture and interpretation. The issue is an allegorical understanding of the Egyptian religion, which aims at taking account of certain interdictions and certain practices. The god Typhon is the sea where the Nile empties and loses itself. "For this reason," writes Plutarch,

the priests abominate the sea and call salt the "spume of
Typhon"; salt is among the foods that must not appear on
their table, and they do not speak to pilots, because these
men make use of the sea, and gain their livelihood from the
sea. This is also one of the principal reasons for their aver-
sion to fish, and it explains why they portray hatred by
drawing the picture of a fish. . . . That saying of the adher-
ents of Pythagoras that "the sea is a tear of Kronos" may
seem to hint at its impure and extraneous nature.[10]

The sea is not of the same race, nor of the same lineage; it
does not correspond: it is the other, the dissonant. A previous chapter, which already brought up abstinence from
fish, concludes thus: "In fine, the priests hold the sea to be
derived from purulent matter, and to lie outside the con-
fines of the world and not to be a part of it or an element,
but a corrupt and pestilential residuum of a foreign
nature."[11] The Greek term used here, *perittôma*, evokes
something excremental, the product of elimination. Is this
the reason why the sea is impure?

The sea is the perpetual testimony in the world of that
which precedes the world, of that upon which and against
which the world was conquered, the waters of chaos that
continue to surround it, the power of the formless, at the
origin as at the end.[12] Beyond limits there extends the
threatening, frightening unlimited. Contrary to so many
other beliefs, here the sea does not constitute the place of
purification through a return to the origin, through a bath
in the origin, but rather the place of an impurity that is
stronger than every determined stain or blemish, for there
is something of the impurity of chaos about it that places
the very existence of whatever form there may be in peril.[13]
But the attaching of the Pythagorean saying about the tear
of Kronos to this interpretation of Egyptian myths seems
artificial, and the lachrymal character of the sterile and
salty sea is not thematized by Plutarch. The situation is
quite different with the Valentinian myth.

The Valentinian myth has the world and the elements that compose it rise up at the end of a powerful and complex divine pre- or protohistory.[14] At the origin, or rather before any origin: the divine Abyss, and its paredrus Silence (this word is feminine in Greek). They produce an entire series of divine principles, proceeding by couples, called the Eons, which constitute the entirety of the divine world, the Pleroma. The last, and the furthest from the Absolute, is Sophia, Wisdom, who shows herself to be rather lacking in wisdom. She wanted to contemplate the invisible Father and grasp the ungraspable. First, and this impossible passion unleashed a series of catastrophes more or less happily compensated for by the Eons. Her passion-related intention, the *Enthumèsis,* detached itself from her and was expelled from the Pleroma, which from that point forward had an outside. Her desire, to become "a new being, a new person," was the Sophia of below, or Achamoth. She suffers in the solitude of darkness and nostalgia for the divine light to which she can in no way return.

The entire range of passions that she experiences will give birth to matter and to the world in which we find ourselves. The witness of Saint Irenaeus of Lyon here is conclusive. But, as Hans Jonas notes, "The correlation of emotions and elements is not fixed in detail but varies considerably from author to author, and probably even within the thought of one and the same author."[15] What does Saint Irenaeus say? "Seeing herself abandoned, alone, outside, she was stricken by all of the elements of this multiple and diverse passion: she experienced sadness for not having taken hold of the light; fear at the prospect of seeing life escape her in the same way as did the light; and anguish on top of all of this."[16] And all of these passions take shape and become a body; the elementary passions form the elements of the world. "From the tears of Achamoth come every wet substance; from her laugh, the luminous substance; from her sadness and her joy, the corporal elements of the world."[17] And Saint Irenaeus of Lyon scoffs at the romanticism of this mythology: "Who then would not spend all his fortune in order to learn that, from the tears of the Enthymesis fallen in passion from the Eon, the seas, the springs, the rivers and every wet substance draw their origin? or that from her laugh comes light?"[18] Tertullian gives the same witness, likewise shot through with irony, in his treatise *Against the Valentinians:*

> You have just heard tell of grief and fear: from these is derived all the rest. In fact, from the tears of Achamoth has flowed the liquid element in its entirety (*universa aquarum natura*). Moreover one can gather an idea of her misfortunes from the quantity and the diversity of tears that she has shed! She had salty tears, she had bitter and fresh ones, hot and cold, and also bituminous and ferruginous. . . . Even the rain that falls from the sky comes from the sobbing squalls of Achamoth, and we thus carefully conserve in our cisterns someone's tears of distress.[19]

Beyond the healthy mood and the legitimate horror that this mythology, which makes the material world the product or the subproduct of a fall, can inspire in a Christian, we must recognize that it does not lack poetic power. The passions here are cosmogenetic. If all water is tears, if all water, in a strict sense, incorporates sadness and is sadness rendered visible and tangible, the sentences of Lamartine quoted earlier take on a completely literal truth. We bathe ourselves in the melancholy of nature, always already weeping, always already inconsolable. One understands why the gnostic would want to uproot himself from this world which, in its very being, is impassioned, and would want to flee "anywhere out of the world."

Many centuries later, in his powerful *Philosophie der Mythologie,* Schelling reinterpreted in his own manner the ancient expression according to which the sea is a "tear of Kronos." Water for him is the first materialization of the divine, the "first catabolism," the first descent and the first relaxation. "Water," he writes, "is, in sum, the first expression of this delight nature feels in becoming nature, in leaving the original tension, abandoning its rigor, and renouncing its obstinacy."[20] It is expansive and fecund. But this is said of the wet in general, and not yet of the bitterness of the sea or of tears. How does water become tears? Poseidon, "God of the wild sea," is, says Schelling, "Kronos become softened, or liquefied, and who, feeling himself surpassed, communicates his moroseness and bitterness to the sea; this is why, incontestably, in certain mystery doctrines, the sea was called, according to a quotation from Plutarch, tears of Kronos." And Schelling goes on to see in these ancient representations much more depth than in

> a flat physics, which sees everything in nature as simple exteriority, or a poor philosophy of spirit that cannot perceive in nature any internal process, but simply a hollow succession of processes. Any of nature's qualities has meaning only to the degree in which it is itself originally sensation. The qualities of things cannot be interpreted mechanically, from outside, but only starting from original impressions that receive, in creation, the very essence of nature. Who can imagine that sulfur, the fetid odor of gases and of volatile metals, or even the inexplicable bitterness of the sea, are merely consequences of an accidental physical mixture? Aren't these substances manifestly the children of fear, of anguish, of moroseness, or of despair?

The philosophy of nature here joins up with gnosticism in the affirmation of a nature deployed and torn apart by immemorial passions. The exterior world itself has an interiority for which we feel sympathy, and which sympathizes with us. As Amiel says in a famous and often misunderstood phrase, the landscape is a state of soul, of the soul of the world. Every journey is sentimental, because, according to these views, we do not project our passions within the world, but rather the passions project themselves into natural forms, wildly.

Why would the sadness of water be only bitterness? Why could it not be mercy? The esotericism of Franz von Baader, in the age of German romanticism, went that far. In the beautiful and dense essay entitled *Sur la notion du temps (On the Notion of Time),* which he wrote directly in a French full of tasty blunders, Baader affirms that the place of the fall can also be that of redemption, and eventually says: "As a consequence *temporal nature shows itself to be the first religion.* It is merciful love that *temporizes* with her lost children, and elemental water, termed by Steffens the tear of nature, can thus be named for the same reason the first tear of this love."[21] It is upon us and toward us that water weeps. And its perpetual descent, its predilection for abasement, which makes Christian authors often see in water the symbol of humility, here becomes the very condescension of love bending down toward the loved being. This is certainly a less cruel vision than that of a nature torn apart by bitter and violent passions.

Upon closing all of these books, should we just forget these marine tears and dry them? What is there to draw from this brief lachrymal anthology? It bears several lessons. First, that the human relation to the elementary is not itself elementary. Between the rumor of the sea and ourselves, between its tears and our own, there will have always been, not a mute face-to-face, but the murmuring, heavy with thousands of words, of our own listening. He who throws himself naked into the sea, as if to commune with it, will not have taken off the glory of the speech that always clothes him, and he plunges in with his word, too, no less supple than his own limbs. This is something that the impoverished opposition of "nature" and "culture," which has been the delight of professors, after having been that of sophists, is powerless to think through. The elements are our oldest archives, but in our archives of words, they too live their own history. Tears of men or tears of the ocean, it is always within the Word that they will have been spilled. To imagine a world without speech, and without the history of this speech, is an empty enterprise, impossible and contradictory.

The second lesson runs counter to certain prejudices. By refusing to make of the world and of its elements, like the ancient cosmogonies or ever-renewed gnosticism, the body or the corporal humor of a god or gods—blood, sperm, saliva, or tears—monotheism inaugurates respect for nature as such and the recognition of its elements as elementary. The Gentiles believe they love nature, and sometimes they worship it, but it is they themselves that they love through it, and not the real sea, nor the real mountains. They do not take these as accomplished, unprecedented works, nor as mute brothers for whom, being together in front of the Unique, we have the responsibility to render incandescent, in our voice, the liberated song.

The third lesson is the first two again. Human art offers its voice to that which has none, and presents to all things that are held prisoner to silence the universal escape of its fragile word. This voice must be offered, and not merely lent. And thus it must listen to that for which we are to be the spokesmen. Certainly, the sea weeps, but need we only taste tears there? Does the sea not also know how to burst into measureless laughter? All analogy is only a path. It reverses itself when it renders the imagination and the attention captive, and makes us hear nothing more than ourselves. Water has more resourcefulness than do our tears; go on, then: to dry your own, rediscover it now.

NOTES

1. Cf. Sudek, *Josef Sudek*, pref. Porter; *Josef Sudek*, pref. Fárová.

2. Verlaine, *Œuvres poétiques complètes*, 122; Bernstein, *Baudelaire, Rimbaud, Verlaine*, 277–78.

3. Bartas, *La sepmaine, ou, Création du monde*, 55.

4. Hildegard of Bingen, *Le livre des œuvres divines*, 90.

5. Cited by Bachelard, *L'eau et les rêves*, 124.

6. Victor Hugo, "La mer et le vent," *Œuvres complètes, Critique*, 681. For the sea's joy, cf. 682: "When the sea wishes, she is merry."

7. Musset, *Poésies complètes*, 273.

8. Augustine, *Contra Adimantum*, XVII:6, in Jolivet and Jourjon, *Six traités anti-manichéens*, 335.

9. Clement of Alexandria, *Stromateis*, V, 8, 50; Porphyry, *Vie de Pythagore*, 41, tran. Places, 55.

10. Plutarch, *De Iside et Osiride*, 32, 363 F-364 A; tran. Babbitt, *Isis and Osiris* in *Moralia*, V, §68, 79–81 [translation modified].

11. Plutarch, *De Iside et Osiride*, 7, 353 E; tran. Babbitt, 19–21. Egypt would have been conquered on the sea by the Nile, water driving back water, the fresh water driving back the salt water (40, 367 B; tran. Babbitt, 99).

12. Cf. Morenz, *Egyptian Religion*, 25–26, 171.

13. Cf. the amazing end of chapter VII of Michelet's *La mer*.

14. Cf. Jonas, *The Gnostic Religion*, 174–97, which we follow in keeping to its broad outline.

15. Ibid., 187.

16. Irenaeus of Lyons, *Adversus haereses*, I, 4, 1; tran. Unger, *Against the Heresies*, 1:30–31 [translation modified].

17. Irenaeus of Lyons, *Adversus haereses*, I, 4, 2; tran. Unger, *Against the Heresies*, 1:31.

18. Irenaeus of Lyons, *Adversus haereses*, I, 4, 3: tran. Unger, *Against the Heresies*, 1:31.

19. Tertullian, *Contre les Valentiniens*, XV, 2–3–4; tran. Fredouille, 116–17, cf. Tertullian, *Contre les Valentiniens*, XXIV, 1–2; tran. Fredouille, 131.

20. Schelling, *Philosophie der Mythologie*, lesson XXV, 581; tran. Pernet, *Philosophie de la mythologie*, 385.

21. Baader, *Sämmtliche Werke*, II:57.

BIBLIOGRAPHY

Anselm. *Monologion.* In *Basic Writings,* translated by S. N. Deane, 2d ed. Chicago and La Salle, Ill.: Open Court, 1962.

Apollinaire, Guillaume. *Chroniques d'art, 1902–1918.* Edited by Leroy Breunig. Paris: Gallimard, 1983.

Arasse, Daniel. *Le détail. Pour une histoire rapprochée de la peinture.* Paris: Flammarion, 1996.

Aristotle. *De Anima.*

———. *Metaphysics.*

———. *Physics.*

Ascione, Gina Carla. *La pittura napoletana dal Caravaggio a Luca Giordano.* Naples: Societa Editrice Napoletana, 1982.

Augustine. *De Civitate Dei (The City of God Against the Pagans).* Translated by R. W. Dyson. Cambridge: Cambridge University Press, 1998.

———. *Contra Adimantum.* In *Six traités anti-manichéens,* translated by Régis Jolivet and Maurice Jourjon. Paris: Desclée de Brouwer, 1961.

———. *Eighty-three different Questions.* Translated by David L. Mosher. Washington, D.C.: Catholic University of America Press, 1977.

———. *In Evangelium Iohannis Tractatus (Tractates on the Gospel of John, 1–10).* Translated by John W. Rettig. Washington, D.C.: Catholic University of America Press, 1988.

———. *In Evangelium Iohannis Tractatus (Tractates on the Gospel of John, 28–54).* Translated by John W. Rettig. Washington, D.C.: Catholic University of America Press, 1993.

_____. *De libero arbitrio.* In *The Teacher, The Free Choice of the Will, Grace and Free Will,* translated by Robert P. Russell, O.S.A. Vol. 59 of *The Fathers of the Church.* Washington, D.C.: Catholic University of America Press, 1968.

_____. *De Trinitate (The Trinity).* Translated by Edmund Hill, O.P. Brooklyn, N.Y: New City Press, 1991.

_____. *De vera religione.* In *Augustine: Earlier Writings,* translated by John H. S. Burleigh. Philadelphia, Pa.: Westminster Press, 1958.

Baader, Franz von. *Sämmtliche Werke.* Leipzig: Bethmann, 1851.

Bachelard, Gaston. *L'eau et les rêves.* Paris: José Corti, 1942.

Barrès, Maurice. *Le mystère en pleine lumière.* Paris: Plon, 1926.

Bartas, Guillaume de Salluste du. *La sepmaine, ou, Création du monde.* Edited by Victor Bol. Arles: Actes Sud, 1987.

Bataille, Georges. "Hegel, la mort, et le sacrifice." In *Œuvres complètes,* Vol. XII. Paris: Gallimard, 1972–88, 326–45. Translated into English as "Hegel, Death and Sacrifice." In *Yale French Studies* 78. New Haven, Conn.: Yale University Press, 1990.

_____. *L'expérience intérieure.* In Vol. V of *Œuvres complètes.* Paris: Gallimard, 1972.

_____. *Manet.* Genève: Skira, 1983. Translated by Austryn Wainhouse and James Emmons. New York: Skira, n.d.

Baudelaire, Charles. *Œuvres complètes.* Edited by Y. G. Le Dantec and Claude Pichois. Paris: Pléiade, 1968.

Beierwaltes, Werner. *Eriugena: Grundzüge seines Denkens.* Frankfurt: Klostermann, 1994.

Bernstein, Joseph M., ed. *Baudelaire, Rimbaud, Verlaine: Selected Verse and Prose Poems.* New York: The Citadel Press, 1947.

Bérulle, Pierre de. *Opuscules de piété.* Edited by Gaston Rotureau. Paris: Aubier/Editions Montaigne, 1944.

Bonaventure. *Breviloquium.* Vol. II of *The Works of Bonaventure.* Translated by José de Vinck. Paterson, N.J.: St. Anthony Guild Press, 1963.

Bourgoing, François. *Méditations sur les vérités et excellences de Jésus-Christ Notre Seigneur: Recueillies de ses mystères, cachées en ses étas et grandeurs; prêchées par lui sur la terre, et communiquées à ses saints.* First published Paris: S. Huré, 1636. Edited by A. M. P. Ingold, Paris, 1892.

Brion, Marcel. *Peinture romantique.* Paris: Albin Michel, 1967.

Brown, Jonathan. *The Golden Age of Painting in Spain.* New Haven, Conn.: Yale University Press, 1991.

Bruyn, Jean-Pierre de. *Le siècle de Rubens dans les collections publiques françaises.* Paris: Editions des musées nationaux, 1977.

Bussière, Sophie de. *Albrecht Dürer. Œuvre gravé (collection Dutuit).* Paris: Edition Paris Musées, 1996.

———. *Rembrandt, Eaux-fortes.* Paris: Edition Paris Musées, 1986.

Carus, Carl Gustav, and Caspar David Friedrich. *De la peinture de paysage dans l'Allemagne romantique.* Translated by Erika Dickenherr et al. Edited by Marcel Brion. Paris: Klincksieck, 1983.

Chardon, Louis. *La croix de Jésus où les plus belles vérités de la théologie mystique et de la grâce sanctifiante sont établies.* 1647. Republished Paris: Editions du Cerf, 1937.

Chrétien, Jean-Louis. *Corps à corps: à l'écoute de l'œuvre d'art (Hand to Hand: Listening to the Work of Art).* Paris: Les Editions de Minuit, 1997.

———. "Joseph Joubert: une philosophie à l'état naissant." In *Revue de métaphysique et de morale* (1979) 4:467–92.

———. *L'Appel et la réponse.* Paris: Editions de Minuit, 1992.

———. *L'Arche de la parole.* Paris: Presses universitaires de France, 1998, 1999.

———. "Pouvoir mourir et devoir mourir selon la théologie chrétienne." In *Le regard de l'amour.* Paris: Desclée de Brouwer, 2000.

———. "La prière selon Kierkegaard." In *Le regard de l'amour.* Paris: Desclée de Brouwer, 2000.

_____. "Retrospection." In *The Unforgettable and the Unhoped For*, translated by Jeffrey Bloechl. New York: Fordham University Press, 2002.

_____. "La traduction irréversible." In Emmanuel Lévinas, *Positivité et transcendance, suivi de Lévinas et la phénoménologie.* Edited by Jean-Luc Marion. Paris: Presses universitaires de France, 2000.

_____. "La vision et l'amour." In *Le regard de l'amour.* Paris: Desclée de Brouwer, 2000.

_____. *La voix nue. Phénoménologie de la promesse.* Paris: Editions de Minuit, 1990.

Cicero. *De natura deorum.* Translated by H. Rackham. London: William Heinemann, Ltd.; New York: G.P. Putnam's Sons, 1933.

Claudel, Paul. *Les aventures de Sophie.* Paris: Gallimard, 1948.

_____. *Cinq grandes odes.* In *Œuvre poétique.* Paris: Pléiade, 1967.

_____. *L'épée et le miroir.* Paris: Gallimard, 1948.

_____. *L'Evangile d'Isaïe.* Paris: Gallimard, 1951.

_____. *Introduction au livre de Ruth.* Paris: Gallimard, 1938.

_____. *Journal.* Paris: Pléiade, 1968.

_____. *Au milieu des vitraux de l'Apocalypse.* Paris: Gallimard, 1966.

_____. *L'Œil écoute.* In *Œuvres en prose.* Paris: Pléiade, 1965. Translated by Elsie Bell as *The Eye Listens.* Port Washington, N.Y.: Kennikat Press, 1950, 1969.

_____. *Œuvres complètes.* 27 vols. Paris: Gallimard, 1950–.

_____. *Œuvre poétique.* Paris: Pléiade, 1967.

_____. *Œuvres en prose.* Paris: Pléiade, 1965.

_____. *Paul Claudel interroge l'Apocalypse.* Paris: Gallimard, 1986.

_____. *Paul Claudel interroge le Cantique des cantiques.* Paris: Gallimard, 1948.

_____. *La rose et le rosaire.* Paris: Gallimard, 1947.

_____. *Le soulier de satin.* In *Théâtre.* Paris: Pléiade, 1965.

_____. *Un poète regarde la Croix.* Paris: Gallimard, 1960.

Claudel, Paul, and J. Madaule. *Connaissance et reconnais-sance, Correspondance, 1929–1954.* Paris: Gallimard, 1996.

Clement of Alexandria. *Protrepticus.*

_____. *Stromateis.*

Curtius, Erwin R. *European Literature and the Latin Middle Ages.* Translated by Willard R. Trask. Princeton, N.J.: Princeton University Press, 1990.

Daix, P., and D. Vallier. *Georges Braque. Rétrospective.* Saint-Paul-de-Vence, 1994, no. 27.

Delacroix, Eugène. *Journal.* Paris: Plon, 1980.

Derrida, Jacques. *Donner la mort.* Paris: Editions Galilée, 1999.

_____. "De l'économie restreinte à l'économie générale: un hegelianisme sans réserve." In *L'Ecriture et la différence.* Paris: Seuil, 1967. Translated by Alan Bass as *Writing and Difference.* Chicago: The University of Chicago Press, 1978.

Desbonnets, T. and D. Vorreux, ed. *Saint François d'Assise, Documents, écrits, et premières biographies.* Paris: Editions franciscaines, 1968.

Descartes, René. *Œuvres philosophiques.* Edited by F. Alquié. Paris: Garnier, 1963.

Descombes, Vincent. *Modern French Philosophy.* Translated by L. Scott-Fox and J. M. Harding. Cambridge: Cambridge University Press, 1980.

_____. *Philosophie par gros temps.* Paris: Ed. de Minuit, 1989.

Diderot, Denis. *Salon de 1765.* Edited by Else Marie Bukdahl and Annette Lorenceau. Paris: Hermann, 1984.

Diels, Hermann, and Walther Kranz, ed. *Die Fragmente der Vorsokratiker,* vol. 1. Berlin: Weidmannsche Verlagsbuchhandlung, 1956.

Doran, P. M., ed. *Conversations avec Cézanne.* Paris: Collection Macula, 1978.

Drevet, Patrick. *Petites études sur le désir de voir.* Paris: Gallimard, 1996.

Duthuit, Georges. *L'image et l'instant.* Paris: José Corti, 1961.

———. *Le musée inimaginable.* Paris: José Corti, 1956.

Eriugena, John Scottus. *Periphyseon.* Edited by I. P. Sheldon-Williams. Dublin: Institute for Advanced Studies, 1972–81.

Ernst, Gilles. *Georges Bataille: Analyse du récit de mort.* Paris: Presses universitaires de France, 1993.

Ficino, Marsilio. *Theologia platonica; Théologie platonicienne de l'immortalité des âmes,* texte critique établi et traduit par Raymond Marcel. Paris: Les Belles Lettres, 1964–70.

Focillon, Henri. *Peintures romanes des églises de France.* Paris: Flammarion, 1967.

———. *La vie des formes.* Paris: Presses Universitaires de France, 1970. Translated by Charles Beecher Hogan and George Kubler as *The Life of Forms in Art.* New Haven, Conn.: Yale University Press, 1942.

Forneris, Jean. *La musique et la peinture, 1600–1900. Trois siècles d'iconographie musicale.* Nice: A.C.M.E., 1991.

Forestier, S., A. Sérullaz, and M. Sérullaz. *Delacroix: peintures et dessins d'inspiration religieuse.* Paris: Ministère de la culture et de la communication, Editions de la Réunion des Musées nationaux, 1986.

Francastel, Pierre. *La figure et le lieu. L'order visuel du Quattrocento.* Paris: Gallimard, 1967.

François de Sales. *Œuvres.* Annecy: J. Niérat, et al., 1904.

Fried, Michael. *Absorption and Theatricality: Painting and Beholder in the Age of Diderot.* Berkeley, Calif.: University of California Press, 1980.

Gieben, Servus. "Saint François dans l'art populaire et l'art graphique." In *Saint François et ses frères* (collection). Paris: Albin Michel, 1991.

Griaule, Marcel. *Dieu d'eau: entretiens avec Ogotemmêli.* Paris: Fayard, 1985.

Grou, Jean Nicholas. *L'intérieur de Jésus et de Marie.* Paris: 1829.

Heidegger, Martin. *Aristotle's Metaphysics Theta, 1–3.* Translated by Walter Brogan and Peter Warnek. Bloomington, Ind.: Indiana University Press, 1995.

Heidegger, Martin. *Basic Writings*. Edited by David Farrell Krell, 2d ed. San Francisco: Harper San Francisco, 1977, 1993.

Held, Julius S. "Rembrandt and the Spoken Word." In *Rembrandt Studies*. Princeton, N.J.: Princeton University Press, 1991:164–83.

Henry, Michel. *Voir l'invisible: Sur Kandinsky*. Paris: Editions François Bourin, 1988.

Hibbard, Howard. *Caravaggio*. New York: Harper and Row, 1983.

Hildegard of Bingen. *Le livre des œuvres divines*. Translated by Bernard Gorceix. Paris: Albin Michel, 1982.

Hollander, Anne. *Seeing Through Clothes*. Berkeley, Calif.: University of California Press, 1993.

Homer, William Innes. *Thomas Eakins: His Life and Art*. New York: Abbeville Press, 1992.

Hugo, Victor. *Œuvres complètes, Critique*. Edited by Jacques Seebacher. Paris: Robert Laffont, 1985.

Humfrey, Peter. *Painting in Renaissance Venice*. New Haven, Conn.: Yale University Press, 1995.

Irenaeus of Lyons. *Adversus haereses*. Translated by Dominic J. Unger, O.F.M. Cap., as *Against the Heresies*. New York: Paulist Press, 1992.

Isidore of Seville. *Etymologiae*.

Jonas, Hans. *The Gnostic Religion: The Message of the Alien God and the Beginnings of Christianity*. 3rd ed. Boston: Beacon Press, 2001.

Joubert, Joseph. *Carnets*. Edited by André Beaunier. Paris: Gallimard, 1955.

Justin Martyr. *Dialogue With Tryphon*. Translated by A. Lukyn Williams as *Justin Martyr, the Dialogue with Trypho*. London: S.P.C.K.; New York: Macmillan, 1930.

Keats, John. *Complete Poems*. Edited by Jack Stillinger. Cambridge, Mass.: The Belknap Press of Harvard University Press, 1978, 1982.

Kojève, Alexandre. *Introduction à la lecture de Hegel*. Paris: Gallimard, 1947.

La Bonnardière, Anne Marie. "La tempête apaisée." In *Saint Augustin et la Bible*. Paris: Beauschesne, 1986.

Lacépède, Bernard Germain Etienne. *Histoire naturelle*. Paris: Furne, 1860.

Laclotte, Michel. *Le siècle de Titien*. Paris: Réunion des musées nationaux, 1993.

Lavergnée, A. Brejon de. *Seicento. Le siècle de Caravage dans les collections françaises*. Paris: Ministère de la culture, de la communication, des grands travaux et du bicentenaire, Editions de la Réunion des musées nationaux, 1988.

Leibniz, Gottfried Wilhelm, Freiherr von. *Essais de théodicée (Theodicy: Essays on the Goodness of God, the Freedom of Man, and the Origin of Evil)*. Translated by Austin Marsden Farrer. La Salle, Ill.: Open Court, 1985.

_____. *Monadologie (Monadology, and other Philosophical Essays)*. Translated by Anne Schrecker. Indianapolis, Ind.: Bobbs-Merrill Co., 1965.

Leiris, Michel. *Le ruban au cou d'Olympia*. Paris: Gallimard, 1981.

Leroy-Jay-Lemaistre, Isabelle. *Musée du Louvre, Nouvelles acquisitions du département des sculptures (1984–1987)*. Paris, 1988.

Lessing, Gotthold Ephraim. *Laocoön: An Essay on the Limits of Painting and Poetry*. Translated by Edward Allen McCormick. Baltimore, Md.: Johns Hopkins University Press, 1984.

Levey, Michael. *Painting and Sculpture in France, 1700–1789*. New Haven, Conn.: Yale University Press, 1993.

Leymarie, Jean. *Balthus*. Geneva: Skira, 1990.

Loyrette, Henri. *Impressionnisme: les origines, 1589–1869*. Paris: Réunion des musées nationaux, 1994.

Lubac, Henri de. *Le mystère du surnaturel*. Paris: Aubier, Editions Montaigne, 1965. Translated by Rosemary Sheed as *The Mystery of the Supernatural*. New York: The Crossroad Publishing Company, 1998.

Mahon, Denis. *Il Guercino.* Bologna: Nuova Alfa Editorale, 1991.

Maldiney, Henri. *Regard, Parole, Espace.* Lausanne: Editions de l'Age d'homme, 1973.

Malebranche, Nicolas. *Méditations chrétiennes et métaphysiques.* Vol. X of *Œuvres complètes.* Paris: Vrin, 1967.

Mallarmé, Stéphane. *Collected Poems.* Edited by Carl Paul Barbier and Gordon Millan. Translated by Henry Weinfield. Berkeley, Calif.: University of California Press, 1994.

_____. *Œuvres complètes.* Edited by Barbier and Millan. Paris: Flammarion, 1983.

Marion, Jean-Luc. *Being Given: Toward a Phenomenology of Givenness.* Translated by Jeffrey L. Kosky. Stanford, Calif.: Stanford University Press, 2002.

_____. *La croisée du visible.* Paris: Presses universitaires de France, 1991, 1996.

_____. *God Without Being.* Translated by Thomas A. Carlson. Chicago: University of Chicago Press, 1991.

_____. *In Excess: Studies of Saturated Phenomena.* Translated by Robyn Horner and Vincent Berraud. New York: Fordham University Press, 2002.

_____. *Prolegomena to Charity.* Translated by Stephen E. Lewis. New York: Fordham University Press, 2002.

Maritain, Jacques. *Art et scolastique.* Paris: Desclée de Brouwer, 1965.

Meiss, Millard. "Sleep in Venice: Ancient Myths and Renaissance Proclivities." In *The Painter's Choice: Problems in the Interpretation of Renaissance Art.* New York: Harper & Row, 1976.

Merleau-Ponty, Maurice. *L'Œil et l'esprit.* Paris: Gallimard Folio, 1964. Translated by Michael B. Smith as "Eye and Mind." In *The Merleau-Ponty Aesthetics Reader: Philosophy and Painting.* Evanston, Ill.: Northwestern University Press, 1993.

Meyer, Laure. *Les maîtres du paysage anglais.* Paris: Terrail, 1992.

Michel, Olivier, and Pierre Rosenberg. *Subleyras.* Catalogue d'exposition. Paris: Ministère de la culture et de la communication, Editions de la Réunion des musées nationaux, 1987.

Michelet, Jules. *La mer.* Paris: Gallimard, 1983.

Mongin, Olivier. *Face au scepticisme (1976–1993): les mutations du paysage intellectuel ou l'invention de l'intellectuel démocratique.* Paris: Ed. de la Découverte, 1994.

Morenz, Siegfried. *Egyptian Religion.* Translated by Ann E. Keep. Ithaca, N.Y.: Cornell University Press, 1973.

Musset, Alfred de. *Poésies complètes.* Edited by Maurice Allemand. Paris: Gallimard, 1967.

Nicholas of Cusa. *De docta ignorantia.* Translated by Jasper Hopkins as *Nicholas of Cusa, On Learned Ignorance, A Translation and an Appraisal of De Docta Ignorantia.* Minneapolis: The Arthur J. Banning Press, 1981.

———. *De venatione sapientiae.* In *Philosophisch-theologische Schriften.* Vol. I. Edited by Leo Gabriel. Vienna: Herder, 1967.

———. *De beryllo.* In *Philosophisch-theologische Schriften.* Vol. III. Edited by Leo Gabriel. Vienna: Herder, 1967.

———. *Idiota de mente.* In *Philosophisch-theologische Schriften.* Vol. III. Edited by Gabriel. Vienna: Herder, 1967.

Nietzsche, Friedrich. *Œuvres philosophiques complètes.* Vol. I, pt. 2 of *Ecrits posthumes, 1870–1873.* Translated by Michel Haar and Marc B. de Launay. Paris: Gallimard, 1975.

Panofsky, Erwin. *Idea: A Concept in Art Theory.* Translated by Joseph J. S. Peake. Columbia, S.C.: University of South Carolina Press, 1968.

Pascal, Blaise. *Pensées.* Translated by A. J. Krailsheimer, rev. ed. Harmondsworth: Penguin Books, 1966, 1995.

Pater, Walter. *The Renaissance: Studies in Art and Poetry.* London: Macmillan and Co., Limited, 1928.

Perse, Saint-John. "Silence pour Paul Claudel." In *La Nouvelle Revue française* 33 (1955):387–91.

Philo. *De praemiis et poenis.* Vol. 8 of *Philo,* translated by F. H. Colson. Cambridge, Mass.: Harvard University Press, 1989.

_____. *De somniis.* Vol. 5 of *Philo,* translated by F. H. Colson and G. H. Whitaker. Cambridge, Mass.: Harvard University Press; London: William Heinemann, 1988.

Pickstock, Catherine. *After Writing: On the Liturgical Consummation of Philosophy.* Oxford: Blackwell Publishers, Ltd., 1998, 1999.

Plato. *Complete Works.* Edited by John M. Cooper. Indianapolis, Ind., and Cambridge, Mass.: Hackett Publishing Company, 1997.

Plotinus. *Enneads.* Vol. 1 of *Plotinus,* translated by A. H. Armstrong. Cambridge, Mass.: Harvard University Press; London: William Heinemann, 1966.

_____. *The Enneads.* Translated by Stephen MacKenna. Harmondsworth: Penguin Books, 1991.

Plutarch. *De Iside et Osiride.* Translated by Frank Cole Babbitt as *Isis and Osiris* in vol. V of *Moralia.* Cambridge, Mass.: Harvard University Press; London: William Heinemann, 1962.

_____. *Lives, Pyrrhus.* Vol. IX of *Lives.* Translated by Bernadotte Perrin. London: William Heinemann, 1968.

_____. *Œuvres morales, V, Isis et Osiris.* Edited and translated by Christian Froidefond. Paris: Les Belles Lettres, 1988.

Ponge, Francis. *Le grand recueil, Lyres.* Paris: Gallimard, 1961.

_____. *Nouveau recueil.* Paris: Gallimard, 1967.

Porphyry. *Vie de Pythagore.* Translated by Edouard des Places. Paris: Les Belles Lettres, 1982.

Proust, Marcel. *A la recherche du temps perdu.* Edited by Jean-Yves Tadié et al. Paris: Pléiade, 1988. Translated by C. K. Scott Moncrieff as *Remembrance of Things Past.* New York: Random House, 1934.

Reverdy, Pierre. *Main d'œuvre.* Paris: Mercure de France, 1964.

Richard, Jean-Pierre. *L'univers imaginaire de Mallarmé.* Paris: Editions du Seuil, 1961.

Rilke, Rainer Maria. *Das Buch der Bilder (The Book of Images)*. Translated by Edward Snow. New York: North Point Press, 1991.

_____. *Duino Elegies*. Translated by J. B. Leishman and Stephen Spender. New York: W. W. Norton & Company, 1963.

Rimbaud, Arthur. *Œuvres complètes*. Edited by Antoine Adam. Paris: Pléiade, 1972.

Rodenbach, Georges. *Choix de poésies*. Paris: Fasquelle, 1949.

Ronsard, Pierre de. *Œuvres complètes*. Edited by P. Laumonier. Paris: Hachette, 1973.

Rosenberg, Pierre. *Chardin 1699–1779*. Catalogue. Cleveland, Ohio: Cleveland Museum of Art and Indiana University Press, 1979.

_____. *La peinture française du XVIIe siècle dans les collections américaines*. Paris: Ministère de la culture, Editions de la Réunion des musées nationaux,1982.

Rosenblum, Robert. *Modern Painting and the Northern Romantic Tradition: Friedrich to Rothko*. New York: Harper & Row, 1994.

Roth, Michael S. *Knowing and History: Appropriations of Hegel in Twentieth-Century France*. Ithaca, N.Y.: Cornell University Press, 1988.

Rubin, James H. *Manet's Silence and the Poetics of Bouquets*. Cambridge, Mass.: Harvard University Press, 1994.

Russell, H. Diane. *Claude Lorrain, 1600–1682*. Catalogue. Washington, D.C.: National Gallery of Art, 1982.

Sabatier, François. *Mirors de la musique. La musique et ses correspondances avec la littérature et les beaux-arts, 1800–1950*. Paris: Fayard, 1995.

Schelling, Friedrich Wilhelm Joseph von. *Philosophie der Mythologie* in *Sämmtliche Werke*, vol. 11, t. 2. Stuttgart and Augsburg: J. G. Cotta, 1857. Translated into French by Alain Pernet as *Philosophie de la mythologie*. Grenoble: J. Millon, 1994.

Schneider, Norbert. *Les natures mortes.* Translated by Françoise Laugier-Morun. Cologne: B Taschen, 1994.

Scholem, Gerschom. *De la création du monde jusqu'à Varsovie.* Paris: Cerf, 1990.

Sérullaz, Maurice. *Les peintures murales de Delacroix.* Paris: Les éditions du Temps, 1963.

Spector, Jack J. *The Murals of Eugène Delacroix at Saint-Sulpice.* New York: College Art Association of America, 1967.

Sterling, Charles. *La nature morte. De l'antiquité au XXième siècle.* New revised ed. Paris: Macula, 1985.

Suárez, Francisco. *Opera omnia.* Edited by Vivès. Paris: Bibliopolum Editorem, 1866.

Sudek, Josef. *Josef Sudek.* Preface by Allan Porter. Zürich: U. Bär Verlag, 1985.

Josef Sudek. Preface by Anna Fárová. Paris: Centre national de la photographie, 1990.

Teresa of Avila. *The Interior Castle.* In *Obras completas.* Madrid: Editorial Católica, 1972. Vol. 2 of *The Collected Works of St. Teresa of Avila.* Translated by Kieran Kavanaugh, O.C.D., and Otilio Rodriguez, O.C.D. Washington, D.C.: ICS Publications, 1980.

Tertullian. *Apology, De Spectaculis.* Translated by Gerald H. Rendall. Cambridge, Mass.: Harvard University Press; London: William Heinemann, Ltd., 1931.

_____. *De baptismo.* In *Tertullian's Treatises Concerning Prayer and Concerning Baptism.* Translated by Alexander Souter. London: S.P.C.K., 1919.

_____. *Contre les Valentiniens.* Translated by Jean-Claude Fredouille. Paris: Cerf, 1980.

Thomas Aquinas. *Summa Theologiae.* In *Basic Writings of Saint Thomas Aquinas.* Translated by the English Dominicans. Edited by Anton C. Pegis. Indianapolis, Ind. and Cambridge, Mass.: Hackett Publishing Company, 1997.

Thuillier, Jacques. *Georges de La Tour.* Paris: Flammarion, 1992.

Tomatis, Alfred. *Ecouter l'univers.* Paris: R. Laffont, 1996.

Vendler, Helen. *The Odes of John Keats.* Cambridge, Mass.: Harvard University Press, 1983.

Verlaine, Paul. *Œuvres poétiques complètes.* Edited by Y. G. Le Dantec. Paris: Gallimard, 1959.

Virgil. *The Aeneid of Virgil.* Translated by Allen Mandelbaum. Berkeley, Calif.: University of California Press, 1981.

Wasserman, Earl R. *The Finer Tone: Keats' Major Poems.* Baltimore, Md.: The Johns Hopkins Press, 1953.

Westermann, Mariët. *Le siècle d'or en Hollande.* Translated by Leymarie. Paris: Flammarion, 1996.

Wilde, Johannes. *Venetian Art from Bellini to Titian.* Oxford: Clarendon Press, 1974.

INDEX

Achamoth, tears of, 159, 160
Adoration of the Shepherds (de La Tour), 46
Adoration of the Shepherds (Domenichino), 46
Against the Valentinians (Tertullian), 160
Amor vincit omnia (Caravaggio), 32, 36
Anselm, Saint, 113
Apollinaire, Guillaume, 36
apostles, 64–71, 76–77
Arcadia (Eakins), 26
Archaic Torso of Apollo (Rilke), 24
Aristotle, 18, 120
  Physics, 34
art, 95–97, 111, 118
  divine, 99, 101–103, 105–108, 113–115, 119
  Ficino on, and nature, 116–117
  Joubet on beauty in, 109–110
  Nicholas of Cusa on, 121
  rivalry with nature, 99–100, 116
  Saint Augustine on, 102–107
artist, xviii, 95, 97–98, 102–103, 111–114
attention, silence of, 48–49

Attributes de la musique, Les (Chardin), 29, 34
Augustine, Saint, xix, 102–107, 109, 111

Baader, Franz von, 161–162
Bachelard, Gaston, 144, 155
Balthus, 90–91
baptism, 147
Barrès, Maurice, 7, 8, 9
Bartas, Guillaume du, 98, 155
Baschenis, Evaristo, 32, 34, 36
Bataille, Georges, x, xii–xiv, 20, 53–56, 86
Baudelaire, Charles, 15, 82, 92
beauty, 98, 101, 102, 106
  call of, xv, xvii
  Joseph Joubet on, 109–110
  Plotinus on, 98–99
Bellini, Giovanni, 66, 68, 69, 74–75
Benedict, Saint, 42–43
Berulle, Cardinal Pierre de, 44, 45
blood, 133, 141–145
body, xvii, 73, 75, 77–78
  as instrument of nudity, 88, 92
  as landscape, 63
  as musical instrument, 27, 30
  and nature, 163
  in sleep, 62, 64

Bonaventure, Saint, xix, 111,
    113–115
Book of Images (Rilke), 1–2
Bourgoing, François, 45
Boy with a Cat (Lanfranco), 91
Braque, Georges, 36–38

Caillebotte, Gustave. *Nu au
    divan*, 85
call of beauty, xv, xvii, xix
Caravaggio, Michelangelo
    Merisi da
    Amore vincit omnia, 32, 36
    Lute Player, The, 32
Carpaccio, Vittore, 66, 67, 69
    Legend of Saint Ursula, 71
Carus, Carl Gustav, 50–51
Cecilia, Saint, 23, 31
Cezanne, Paul, 57
    *Modern Olympia (Une mod-
    erne Olympia)*, 86
Chapel of the Angels
    (Delacroix), xiv, 7–15
Chardin, Jean Baptiste
    Simeon, 20, 34, 35
    Les attributes de la musique,
    29
Chardon, Louis, 5–6
charity, 140
Charon, 81–84
*Charon passant les ombres sur le
    Styx* (Subleyras), 81–84
*Christ Embracing Saint Bernard
    in His Arms* (Ribalta), 41
Christ in the Olive Garden (El
    Greco), 65
Christ in the Olive Garden
    (Jordaens), 70
*Christ sur le lac de Genesarteth,
    Le* (Delacroix), 77

Cicero, 100–101
circularity of life, 139
clarity of the work of art, 97,
    99, 105
Claudel, Paul, xix, 19, 125,
    130–139, 141–148
Clement of Alexandria, Saint,
    157
Coccapani, Sigismondo, 40
consciousness of self, x
contemplation, 44
Corot, Jean Baptiste Camille,
    38
Courbet, Gustave, 64
creation, xviii, 102, 119–124,
    139
    artistic, 117
    distinguished from produc-
    tion, 96–97, 105
    divine, 95, 104, 111, 124
    of a work of art, 94
Cupidon assis (Falconet), 28

death, x, xii–xiii, xiv
Delacroix, Eugene, x, xiii–xv,
    xviii, 6–16, 65
    *Christ sur le lac de
    Genesarteth, Le*, 77
de La Tour, Georges.
    Adoration of the Shepherds,
    46
Derrida, Jacques, x, xii–xiii
Descartes, René, 144
desire, 136–137, 139
Diderot, Denis, 34–35
discursivity, 56
Domenichino. *Adoration of the
    Shepherds*, 46
Dream of Jacob (Ribera), 71–72
dreams, represented in art, 71,
    72

Drevet, Patrick, 48
Drunkeness of Noah, The (Bellini), 74–75
Dürer, Albrecht, 70

Eakins, Thomas. *Arcadia*, 26
Eriugena, John Scottus, 111–112
eternity, 146
events, xvii, xviii

faith, 5
Falconet, Etienne Maurice. *Cupidon assis*, 28
Ficino, Marsilio, 113, 115–120
Flûte de Pan (Picasso), 27
Forgotten Ariettas (Ariettes oubliées) (Verlaine), 154
Francis of Assisi, Saint, 38–43
François de Sales, Saint, 5
Frédeau, Ambroise. *Saint Nicolas of Tolentine Lulled by the Angels' Concert*, 43
Friedrich, Caspar David, 50–53

Gaze Into the Beyond (Hodler), 53
Gaze of Silence (Messiaen), 46
Giorgione, 24, 36
God, xix, 73, 102, 106, 146
    as artist, xviii, 95, 99, 103, 111–112
    bond between creatures and, 142–143, 148
    as craftsman, 95–96, 101
    as creator, xviii, 119
    thirst for, 135, 138, 139–140
grace, 31, 132–133

Greco, El. *Christ in the Olive Garden*, 65
Gris, Juan, 37
Grou, Jean Nicholas, 46
Guercino. *Saint Francis and Saint Benedict with an Angel Musician*, 42

handicrafts, 94
hands, work of the, 124, 125
heaven, 147–148
Hegel, Georg Wilhelm Friedrich, ix, xi, xii
Heidegger, Martin, 124
Heliodorus Driven From the Temple (Delacroix), 7, 12, 13
Hildegard of Bingen, 155
Hodler, Ferdinand. *Gaze Into the Beyond*, 53
Hugo, Victor, 156

instruments, musical, 31, 32, 34
    function of, in allegory, 36
instruments of nudity, 85–93
intimacy, 27
Irenaeus of Lyon, Saint, 157, 159, 160

Jacob's ladder, 72
Jacob's struggle, xii–xiv, xvii, xviii, 2–15, 72
Jacob's Wrestling with the Angel (Delacroix), 12
Jesus Christ, 44–47, 64–70, 76, 115
Jeune garçon au chat, Le (Renoir), 87–88
Jordaens, Jacob. *Christ in the Olive Garden*, 70
Joubet, Joseph, 109–111

Keats, John, 21–22, 23, 24
know-how, 96, 117, 118, 120
Kojève, Alexandre, ix, x
Kronos, tear of, 157–158, 160,
161

Lacépède, Bernard Germain
Etienne, 135
Lamartine, Alphonse de,
155–156, 160
landscape
impact of the art of the,
67–69
painting, 25, 51
as state of the soul, 161
in Sudek's photography,
153
Lanfranco, Giovanni. *Boy with
a Cat* , 91
Legend of Saint Ursula
(Carpaccio), 71
Leibniz, Gottfried, 118
Le Seur, Eustache. *Sleeping
Venus Surprised By Love*, 78
Leyster, Judith. *Self-Portrait*, 25
liquid bond, 142–144, 148
listening, act of, 35, 42, 50, 57
to art, xvii, 19
to the invisible, 39
to nature, 27
to paintings, xvi
to silence, 22, 24, 40
listening, dramatic, xiii
Lorrain, Claude, 25–26
Fête villageoise, 26
*Pastoral Landscape with
Piping Shepherd*, 26
love, 5
Lute Player, The (Caravaggio),
32

Malebranche, Nicolas, 114
Mallarmé, Stéphane, 23, 29, 37
Manet, Edouard, 20, 21, 53–56
Olympia, 85–86
Mantegna, Andrea, 66, 68, 69
Master-Slave dialectic, ix, xi
Messiaen, Olivier. *Gaze of
Silence*, 46
*Modern Olympia (Une moderne
Olympia)*(Cezanne), 86
music
abandonment of, 31–32
angelic, 38–43
in painting, 21, 25
silent, 21–22, 33, 35–38, 43,
57
Musset, Alfred de
Namouna, 92
Rolla, 156
*Mystery of Jesus, The (Le mys-
tère de Jésus)* (Pascal), 66
mythology
Egyptian, 157–158
of sleep, 64
Valentinian, 158–159

Namouna (Musset), 92
nature, 27, 51, 68, 160–162
act of listening and, 50
art and, 99–101
liberation from one's own,
xi
silence of, 25
negativity, xii, xix
Nicholas of Cusa, 113, 121–123
Nietzsche, Friedrich, 134
Noah, 73–74
Nu au divan (Caillebotte), 85
nudity, instruments of, 85–93

Ode on a Grecian Urn (Keats),
21–22, 23
Olympia (Manet), 85–87
On Happiness (Plotinus), 30
*On the notion of time (Sur la
notion du temps)* (Baader),
162

painting, xvi, xvii, 18, 31, 64
of absorption, 48
and act of listening, 24
interrogative, 20
music in, 21, 25
silence of, 19–21
Pascal, Blaise, 66–67
Passage du Styx. (Patinir), 82
Pater, Walter, 24, 36
Patinir, Joachim. *Passage du
Styx*, 82
Perse, Saint-John, 146
Petite Tombe, La (Rembrandt),
49
Philo of Alexander, 4
Philosophie der Mythologie, 160
Physics (Aristotle), 34
Picasso, Pablo, 37
Flûte de Pan, 27
Trois musiciens masqués, 36
Plato, 99–100, 148
Platonists, xviii, 108
Plotinus, 31, 98, 99
On Happiness, 30
Plutarch, 28, 157, 158
poetry, 18, 92, 123
Charon in, 81–82
literature and, 62
of tears, 154–155
of water, 131–132
Ponge, Francis, 34–35, 130–131
Préault, Auguste, 28

presence, manual act of, x,
xiv–xv, xv, xvii, xxv
Prisonnière, La (Proust), 62
production, 101, 102, 118, 119
distinguished from cre-
ation, 105
work of art and, 96, 98
Proust, Marcel. *La Prisonnière*,
62
Pythagoras, 157–158

Raphael. *Saint Cecilia*, 31
redemption, 162
*Reign of silence (Regne du
silence)* (Rodenbach), 33
Rembrandt van Rijn, 49–50,
72, 76
La Petite Tombe, 49
Renoir, Pierre Auguste. *Le
jeune garçon au chat*, 87–88
response, xxvi, 57
to beauty, xv, xvii, xix
as translation, xxiii
to work of art, xviii, xxv
Reverdy, Pierre, 124–125
Ribalta, Francisco. *Christ
Embracing Saint Bernard in
His Arms*, 41
Ribera, José. *Dream of Jacob*,
71–72
Rilke, Rainer Maria, 1–2, 4–5,
24, 108
Rimbaud, Arthur, 123, 149
Rodenbach, Georges. *Reign of
Silence (Regne du silence)*, 33
Rolla (Musset), 156

sadness, 160–161
Saint Cecilia (Raphael), 31

Saint Francis and Saint Benedict with an Angel Musician (Guercino), 42
Saint Nicolas of Tolentine Lulled by the Angels' Concert (Frédeau), 43
Saraceni, Carlo, 42
satisfaction, 2
Schelling, Friedrich, 160–161
sea, 140–141, 146–148, 156–160, 163
drinking of the, 136–137
self-abandonment, xiv, 76
self-consciousness, x
self-love, x
Self-Portrait (Leyster), 25
self-understanding, xv
Semaine ou la création du monde, La, 155
silence, xvi, 18–57
sign of, 29
Silence (Préault), 28
sleep, 62–78
Sleeping Venus Surprised by Love (Vénus endormie surprise par l'Amour) (Le Seur), 78
soul, 112
landscape as state of the, 161
as organizer, 100
song of the, 30–31
speech, xxv, 44, 78, 140, 162
dramatic, xvii–xviii, xix
of tears, 152, 156
spiritual scale, 52
still life painting, 34, 42
musical instruments in, 29, 32, 36, 38

Stoicism, 100–101
Subleyras, Pierre, 36, 81–84
Sudek, Josef, 153–154
Suzanne, Saint, 36

tears, 152–163
of the Virgin Mary, 141
Teresa, of Avila, Saint, 132
Tertullian, 130, 157, 160
Thales of Miletus, 134
Theologia platonica (Ficino), 115–120
thirst, 135–138, 140
Thomas Aquinas, Saint, 97, 104
Titian. *Venus of Urbin*, 86

Ursula, Saint, 71

Venus of Urbin (Titian), 86
Verbum infans, 44, 46
Verlaine, Paul. *Forgotten Ariettas (Ariettes oubliees)*, 154
Veronese, Paolo, 71
violence, ix, x, xv, 15, 75

water, 10–11, 130–149, 160–163
bond of blood and, 142–145
waters, higher, 146, 148
work of art, xv, xviii, 94, 114, 124
artist superiority over, 113
clarity of the, 98, 104
making of a, 97
wounds, x, 2, 4

Zeno of Cittium, 100–101
Zurbaran, Francisco de, 46

PERSPECTIVES IN CONTINENTAL PHILOSOPHY SERIES
John D. Caputo, series editor

1. John D. Caputo, ed., *Deconstruction in a Nutshell: A Conversation with Jacques Derrida.*
2. Michael Strawser, *Both / And: Reading Kierkegaard—From Irony to Edification.*
3. Michael D. Barber, *Ethical Hermeneutics: Rationality in Enrique Dussel's Philosophy of Liberation.*
4. James H. Olthuis, ed., *Knowing* Other-*wise: Philosophy at the Threshold of Spirituality.*
5. James Swindal, *Reflection Revisited: Jürgen Habermas's Discursive Theory of Truth.*
6. Richard Kearney, *Poetics of Imagining: Modern and Postmodern.* Second edition.
7. Thomas W. Busch, *Circulating Being: From Embodiment to Incorporation—Essays on Late Existentialism.*
8. Edith Wyschogrod, *Emmanuel Levinas: The Problem of Ethical Metaphysics.* Second edition.
9. Francis J. Ambrosio, ed., *The Question of Christian Philosophy Today.*
10. Jeffrey Bloechl, ed., *The Face of the Other and the Trace of God: Essays on the Philosophy of Emmanuel Levinas.*
11. Ilse N. Bulhof and Laurens ten Kate, eds., *Flight of the Gods: Philosophical Perspectives on Negative Theology.*
12. Trish Glazebrook, *Heidegger's Philosophy of Science.*
13. Kevin Hart, *The Trespass of the Sign: Deconstruction, Theology, and Philosophy.*
14. Mark C. Taylor, *Journeys to Selfhood: Hegel and Kierkegaard.* Second edition.
15. Dominique Janicaud, Jean-François Courtine, Jean-Louis Chrétien, Michel Henry, Jean-Luc Marion, and Paul Ricœur, *Phenomenology and the "Theological Turn": The French Debate.*
16. Karl Jaspers, *The Question of German Guilt.* Introduction by Joseph W. Koterski, S.J.
17. Jean-Luc Marion, *The Idol and Distance: Five Studies.* Translated with an introduction by Thomas A. Carlson.

18. Jeffrey Dudiak, *The Intrigue of Ethics: A Reading of the Idea of Discourse in the Thought of Emmanuel Levinas*.
19. Robyn Horner, *Rethinking God As Gift: Marion, Derrida, and the Limits of Phenomenology*.
20. Mark Dooley, *The Politics of Exodus: Søren Keirkegaard's Ethics of Responsibility*.
21. Merold Westphal, *Toward a Postmodern Christian Faith: Overcoming Onto-Theology*.
22. Edith Wyschogrod, Jean-Joseph Goux and Eric Boynton, eds., *The Enigma of Gift and Sacrifice*.
23. Stanislas Breton, *The Word and the Cross*. Translated with an introduction by Jacquelyn Porter.
24. Jean-Luc Marion, *Prolegomena to Charity*. Translated by Stephen E. Lewis.
25. Peter H. Spader, *Scheler's Ethical Personalism: Its Logic, Development, and Promise*.
26. Jean-Louis Chrétien, *The Unforgettable and the Unhoped For*. Translated by Jeffrey Bloechl.
27. Don Cupitt, *Is Nothing Sacred? The Non-Realist Philosophy of Religion: Selected Essays*.
28. Jean-Luc Marion, *In Excess: Studies of Saturated Phenomena*. Translated by Robyn Horner and Vincent Berraud.
29. Phillip Goodchild, *Rethinking Philosophy of Religion: Approaches from Continental Philosophy*.
30. William J. Richardson, S.J., *Heidegger: Through Phenomenology to Thought*.
31. Jeffrey Andrew Barash, *Martin Heidegger and the Problem of Historical Meaning*.